A
SEARCH
FOR
COLLECTION

A SEARCH FOR COLLECTION

Science and Art in Riding

PAUL BELASIK

J. A. ALLEN

© *Paul Belasik 2009*
First published in Great Britain 2009

ISBN 978 0 85131 965 0

J.A. Allen
Clerkenwell House
Clerkenwell Green
London EC1R 0HT

www.halebooks.com

J.A. Allen is an imprint of Robert Hale Limited

The right of Paul Belasik to be identified as author
of this work has been asserted by him in accordance
with the Copyright, Designs and Patents Act 1988

A catalogue record for this book is available from the British Library

Design by Judy Linard
Photographs 1, 2 and 3 by Karl Leck, 4, 6 and 7 by Belasik Video Associates
and 5 and 8 by Paul Belasik
Edited by Martin Diggle
Printed in China

Contents

CHAPTER 1

Learning to Choose Beautifully

You are born with amnesia. People try to fill in the blanks. Who you are. What you are. What you are supposed to do. They try to do this by telling you stories of who your grandfather was. What your grandfather was. Where your mother grew up. What your father did for a living. All this biography may not help you, because you are unique. No one exactly like you was ever here before. You are not one of those people. I am not one of those people. You are a different person. I am a different person. Who are we? How do we find out?

The people who live here said that December was wetter than normal; as a result now, in January, the island is even more lush than usual. There are dressage horses in Hawaii. In part I'm here on holiday and I will also teach a couple of clinics on two of the islands. Since I am out of my usual routine of horse work, I run into town and back in the mornings for exercise.

Yesterday there was a storm with winds so strong they knocked out power on parts of the island near the volcano. This morning it is tropically beautiful again. Doves and pigeons hypnotically sound their plaintive low pipe notes. The narcotic perfume of plumeria and tube roses hangs in the air, which feels like lotion on your face. In the sky, luxuriant mountain slopes start falling steeply out of their personal clouds; bright green vegetation and wispy white steam patches cling to the descending knife edges, all the way down to a mascara line of road that seems to form a boundary as far as you can see at the blue surf's edge. The slopes don't stop there; they keep falling into the clear blue water. Coral replaces bushes; the surface of the mountain is now bathed in warm water instead of warm air. The sight of birds flying in the air is replaced by turtles and fish that fly in the water. Instead of the tones of elegiac doves, you hear the sonorous distant haunting cello sounds of hump-backed whales. Eventually the slope bottoms out and, miles away, it rises back up again, breaking through the surf into air somewhere to become another island with its own culture and even its own climate.

It is ironic, I think, as I run into town, that when you are inside the water, under the sea, you cannot smell the beautiful fragrances created by the water. Your senses place you and help define you, exalt you and, in the end, limit you. It is interesting how the sense of smell, the olfactory lobe in the brain itself and the cells that analyse smell, are the ancient root of our emotional life.[1]

Toward town I run past a church, all the doors and windows wide open. The definition of living or doing something inside or outside is so blurry here. The varnished, immaculate wood shines inside. In front, a man rakes palm fronds that were shaken

[1] D. Goleman, *Emotional Intelligence*, Bantam Books, 1995.

down from the coconut tree onto the perfect lawn. I pass the elementary school with its open rooms, the playground is quiet – all the young students are in their classes, knapsacks hanging evenly in rows outside each classroom door. I wonder what kind of torture it is to be stuck in there, when on one side, in plain sight, are surfers, fishermen, whales breeching, and on the other side, mountains with blasting streams and steamy jungles full of animal spirits. I am not sure I understand school at all anymore; what is its real purpose?

A little further on, I go through the town square with its magnificent banyan tree, with arms that grow out hundreds of feet and arch back into the ground to become roots again – or is it roots that grow up out of the ground to become branches that make sweeping searches for the ground again? In being whatever it is, it leaves a maze of great arbour-shaded rooms, where artisans come to sell their work on the weekends under the live, bushy ceiling filled with a thousand chattering birds. I continue past the sea wall where several Hawaiians are fishing and then past a few more shops which thin out as I am on the other side of town. I turn around and head back. On the way home I lose my seriousness and drop down to a walk, detouring over to the wharfs where charter boats are preparing to go out. The light smell of diesel exhaust puffs over the dock. I see a small surf shop; there is a pile of used boards for sale stacked on top of each other. From a distance the smooth, shiny, interlocked white pile looks like the great weathered vertebrae that might mark the door of some ancient whaling shack. When I get there the door is open; I go inside. There is a young bohemian couple sitting on a beaten-up old couch intently watching a video on a small television. He tells me it's a documentary about surfing thirty years ago. I know they have seen this film many times. Still they study it. The same way I have studied riding films, sometimes not even knowing what you are looking for, just watching for a sign, a clue, something to be revealed, sometimes watching a favourite moment over and over again, memorizing it.

I have been watching the surfers for a while; the young ones begin self-sculpting, seeing what their flesh, bones and the sea water will yield.

Suppose, whatever way it comes to you, it comes to you that you cannot see any difference between going to Harvard University and filling the vacancies of big businesses and governments or going to Hamburger University and filling the vacancies of McDonald's. Somehow, it has come to you that your life is not a design project for someone else. The answer to who I am and what I am supposed to do cannot be satisfied by an address, a birth certificate or a social security number. To start to find out what to do with your life, you cannot go to a society whose primary goal is to homogenize minds so that they can easily be mobilized for its wars: class wars, school wars, gang wars, religious wars, corporate wars, world wars. Like a rat before a baited trap, you can feel this poison of propaganda with your whiskers, so you stay hungry and wonder.

The answer to who you are must be closer to such questions as: 'Am I fearful?' 'Am I cautious?' 'Am I reckless or bold?' 'Am I compassionate?' 'Am I sick or am I well?' When Sun Yat Sen wrote *The Art of War*, he should have written that the first battle will be to rid yourself of the guilt that will be put upon you as you go to work on yourself, and that this does not mean you are excluding all others. A psychological affirmation is not a societal rejection. If you want to know who you are and what you are supposed to do, you cannot really go even to the people who love you. It may be that they would rather see you safe than self-fulfilled. Mothers and fathers, families with mental or physical histories to uphold or redeem, pick acceptable careers and start you up a fish weir when you are very young. You get so far that you can't be ungrateful and waste everything that has placed you where you are, so you die a little and begin to wonder if something else was really meant for you. You alter reality, because the reality presented to you is not real to you.

If you want to know something about yourself, you can't start by asking someone who has a stake in the outcome. If you are a surfer, you go to the ocean. Nature is not a nation. Nature is not beneficent or cruel. It doesn't care how much money you have, or what your pedigree is. It can present you with every range of power to test yourself. You can control just how much you want to learn. Nature has no stake in the outcome. Whatever you ask, the answer will be pure. If you go beyond your limits you will pay; if you stay under your limits all the time, your spirit and body will wither and weaken. To find out about yourself, to collect your own experiences, you will have to stay out on the ocean for a long time. In order to stay out there and not be killed, you will need technique. You will gain technique through practice. Through practice you will learn how to choose beautifully.

So my friends the surfers always go to the ocean, and my friends the riders have always gone to the horses; many of us have been hurt, and some even killed. As time goes by for me, two groups seem to have developed. For one, the principle connection will always be to other human beings. These people need external evaluation and validation. For them, to do a thing undocumented or unnoticed is not to do a thing at all. Who they are is always answered by other people – often people they don't know. If lovers and therapists, enemies and friends – not an ocean or a horse – answer your questions, over a long time the birthright of your amnesia is superficially sated with a persona built upon cross-examinations of other people, held together by outside opinion. Yet, even if they do a good job, from time to time – in faint dreams, like a Zen *koan* – you wonder if you have a personality if no one is around and, deep inside, things still wobble a little if your describers fall down on the job. Obsolete rat whiskers, like phantom pain for an amputee, once in a while stir, but are quickly rationalized out of existence.

But there is the other group, and this group seems to fall in love with motion itself. They resist interpretations and explanations of what they do by other people. They need direct experience, and are suspicious when it is evaluated, translated, analysed, rewarded or punished. When you almost drown, no one has to tell you made a mistake; when you get thrown from a horse and break your ribs, no one has to explain the pain. It's up to you to find out why, and whether you can do something better next time.

Like Don Quixote with his concussion, these people must find out every day who they are; their amnesia is not sated because they are not defined by anyone. They can have many names and at the same time they don't seem to need any of them. They are like water, they are like horses; they change. Maybe they never had amnesia at all but they were told they did, over and over and over, so they would forget the possibilities.

CHAPTER 2

The Culture of Horses – 'The Thin Layer of Domestication'

People oversimplify equine behaviour. They oversimplify their relationships with horses. They anthropomorphize. For the greatest part of our historical relationship, people have tried to conquer horses. De Pluvinel suggested a different approach; was he realistic? At first glance it seems that the lives of horses are violence-based. If this is so, this would trigger some complicated philosophical discussions in regard to their training. Horses exist in hierarchies, not democracies. Some are dominant, some submissive. The dominant ones eat and drink first. How do they do this? In the end, where do they get their authority? How do they enforce their will? Certainly, one way they do it is with strength, with actual or perceived violence. At the bottom of all the talk, does this mean that horse relationships are fear-based? In order to get them to do what we want, is this what we must acknowledge? Dominant horses will, at some time – and maybe many times – be challenged. If they don't back down their

13

challengers, they lose their status. They may be taking orders instead of giving them.

Most riders never get to feel collection, they never get to try the things they have read about or seen, that they want to feel so badly. The limitations are not usually the rider's intelligence or their athletic ability. The limits are their relationships with their horses. They choose badly. They lead badly. Their horse, like a politically occupied country, is so full of resistance that the simplest tasks of governing are impossible, much less the complex ones. In a sense, there are a lot of prerequisites for learning collection and they are not all requirements of riding skill or theory, or of science. They are first about finding a partner and understanding how to work with him.

So, what kind of animals are horses? How can we hope to train them unless we understand something about the motivations of their behaviour, their natural tendencies, and their psychology?

In order to find out more about horses in their natural state, I contacted Dr. Jay Kirkpatrick, who is a world authority on wild horses. Dr. Kirkpatrick lives in Montana most of the year; we talked about observing the mustangs out west in the Pryor Mountains and so on. He said that could be difficult, as the snow might not be passable until June and, because of the range the horses covered, we might not see horses for days. He suggested instead that I come to Assateague Island off the east coast of Maryland in March. He has spent several months there for many years in charge of keeping the wild horse population inside the seashore National Park at a sustainable level. He has done this by developing an elegant system that involves darting different mares each year with a contraceptive. He has to get within fifty yards of the target mare to be successful. He told me later that he has used this system with different animals all over the world, that he has stalked even white-tailed deer, but that horses are so perceptive he has never been able to stalk a wild horse. One of the first things you should know about horses is that as soon as you have come into their picture, you are being observed.

It is interesting that a great deal of work on feral horses comes from studying the populations of wild horses that inhabit a long, thin string of islands off the central and south-eastern coast of the United States, Assateague being the northern-most part, in the state of Maryland. The islands, and therefore the herds of horses that live on them, run under different federal, state and local jurisdictions. Depending on the quality and philosophy of the managers, certain places may be overpopulated with horses competing for limited resources.

It is not perfectly clear how it is that horses came to inhabit these islands. Some people have said they are descendants of horses that survived shipwrecks from the time of the first settling of the Americas. Other theories propose that, in order for early settlers to escape taxation, they hid livestock on the islands; horses escaped and thrived there, in spite of an extremely harsh environment. The islands have scarce fresh water. Sometimes, at first sight of the horses, they seem fat but this is not a result of lush food sources, but rather bloated bellies that result from the horses drinking volumes of brackish water in order to quench their thirst. In the winter the horses can be seen eating poison ivy; the food is not exactly rich. In the summer the marshlands and temperatures form incubators for swarms of vicious biting, bloodsucking flies and mosquitoes, which prompt these horses to sometimes spend hours hiding in the sea water.

In spite of these conditions, they have thrived on these islands for over 300 years and, in this limited space, scientists have had an amazing laboratory to study the behaviour of horses.

I had set up a day to meet Jay and interview him for a film we were making about horses, so a small film crew and I headed down to the National Park. Since none of us had been there before we decided to start down the day before to scout out the place and make sure we weren't late the next morning. It was nearly dusk when we arrived at the park headquarters but, since there was still a little daylight left, the crew wanted to test the cameras and have a look around the tip of the island. We crossed a small bridge onto the island. Within a few hundred yards of the bridge we saw our first wild horse, an immaculately clean paint horse standing all alone, grazing quietly on the ocean's edge with a low moon hanging in the sky behind him. We went further out onto the island and could see small bands of horses way out on the marshes. It was a beautiful, peaceful sight. A front was coming in and by the next day the weather would turn raw. After all, it was March. I would soon learn that the idyllic life of the horses was about to change, as with the spring came the rise in sun and with it the rising of hormones. The 'horse wars' were about to begin.

The amazing coincidence is that when the question of horses' intelligence would come up, Jay would tell us that very first horse we saw that night, who was named Scotty, was legendary for his feats of intelligence. Scotty, it turns out, was old now; he had lost his band of mares and was living out his last days alone – and horses don't last long alone. In his prime, to protect his mares, Scotty would herd them up the road between the guardrails of the causeway and patrol the short section in front, making it impossible for any interloper to get past him to the mares. Another of his famous ploys came about because part of the island was a National Park and many visitors came to camp in the good weather. The wild horses were a nuisance. In spite of rules not to feed the horses, the visitors loved the interaction and couldn't care less if the odd tent was pulled over: it only added to their vacation stories. The park took a less enthusiastic view of these encounters with wild animals, so they built a large corral, only this corral was for campers to go in and keep the horses out; it had access to freshwater, etc. Of course, no one really wanted to be separated from the horses so it was eventually abandoned – until Scotty figured that he could herd the mares in there. There was grass to eat, fresh water to drink and all he had to do was guard a small gateway, which was the only access to his band. Jay told me that while other stallions were constantly on guard worrying about keeping each other from stealing mares from a perpetually moving group, Scotty would fall asleep in the opening; any challenger would literally have to step over him to get to the mares. Breeding rights don't go just to the strongest horses; they go to the smartest as well. Horses, it seems, can survey surroundings and extrapolate new creative uses of existing situations. Horses are perceptive and very intelligent.

In the morning, the front had come through; it made outdoor filming difficult. We started with the interview and Jay began to take us through some of the science of the personalities of some of the notable horses on Assateague. With the rising of the spring sun will come the rising of hormones: testosterone in stallions and oestrodiol in mares. With these comes a marked increase in aggression toward other horses and even toward people. This hormonal rise has been quantified by a simple little test. When mares' hormones rise, they will be present in her urine. If the stallion comes up to a spot of urination he has the potential to do five things. One, go to the site of the mare's elimination. Two, he will sniff the elimination. Three, he will turn his upper lip, curling it towards his nostrils, in what is called the Flehman display. Four, he can urinate on the site and five, defecate on the site. An observer will score the stallion. As the sun keeps rising, by May the stallion might do all five, whereas in November, when the mares' hormones are not so strongly present and his own testosterone level has decreased, he may do only one or two. It would not do for a successful population to just have indiscriminate breeding. So, with the hormones comes of whole gamut of societal behaviours that end up selecting breeding horses. To say that only the strongest or most aggressive will breed is not accurate. Horses like Scotty are simply smarter and more creative.

Early behaviourists apparently confused dominance and aggression. To give an example of aggression, Dr. Kirkpatrick told us about two horses, one called Hot Air Balloon, and another called Smudge. Hot Air Balloon was one of the most aggressive horses the island had ever seen. He picked a fight with everyone, but he never won a fight. Smudge was always laid-back; he never started a fight, but if someone else did, he never lost. There could be aggressive dominant horses but there could be aggressive submissive horses. Aggression was not necessarily linked to dominance, nor was it necessarily a successful breeding or leading strategy.

Dominance itself is also enigmatic. Dominant horses always eat first or drink first. In my own band of broodmares, Denali is the dominant mare; she always eats first and drinks first. The other mares barely challenge her, yet she is not aggressive; she rarely even moves an ear. It's understood. Dominant horses are not necessarily leaders, but they can be. Horse personalities are complex – the more you understand the individual, the more you can predict their behaviour and, in training, modify the outcome. For scientists like Dr. Kirkpatrick, the intriguing question is whether the dominance is learned or is a genetic trait. He told us the story of an amazing stallion who recently died. His name was 9NH. Normally stallions do not acquire a band until they are at least 6 or 7 years old, but often it can be 9 or 10 and, even when they are as smart as Scotty was, when they get older they will be deposed. However, 9NH acquired his first band when he was only 4 years old and he held that band until the day he died when he was over 20 years old. The interesting thing here is that 9NH's mother was 9N and she was one of the most dominant mares ever observed on the island. Dominant horses may inherit dominance or they may learn it. The evidence seems to point to a combination of nature and nurture.

Finally, leadership seems to be another category altogether. Leadership isn't necessarily attached to aggression, and it isn't necessarily attached to dominance. It does seem to be connected to intelligence or creativity. To me, this whole passion play is rather ingenious because it does not put the future of the population into the hands of one particular attribute. It's almost as if what nature looks for is ways for the smartest and the strongest horses to improve the population, to use all the best traits.

It's also clear in breeding that stallions are not the major players that most people think – mares select the stallion. One of the strongest forces of all in the horse's life is the need to be together. Horses are extremely social. The mares will accept a stallion who can accommodate that. If one seems disruptive or too weak to ward off intruders, who will break up the band, they might leave him undefended until he is bloodied and bowed, beaten by relentless challengers. Leadership does not appear to be something that can be thrust upon the population – how it is first accepted may not be exactly known – but that it can be deposed, withdrawn, if the leader makes bad choices, is a fact.

Two mares who have never met approach each other. One is introducing herself to a pre-existing band. The new mare approaches the current dominant mare in the band. They stand parallel, nose to tail, each strongly sniffing the flank of the other. It seems innocuous, but anyone who has seen this situation knows not to stand too close. In a second, there is a loud squeal; one of the mares strikes the ground hard with a foreleg. The new mare wheels around in a small semi-circle trying to position her rump towards the dominant mare to threaten a kick. The dominant mare doesn't yield any ground, but quickly turns slightly and scores a direct hit with both hind feet on the muscular rump of the new animal. The new mare is furious, she flattens her ears back against her head, curls her lips back, bares her teeth and charges, snaking her neck from side to side toward the dominant mare. The dominant mare does not move; she seems almost oblivious. The new mare charges but she is twenty feet away. She kicks with both hind feet in the direction of the older mare. She is conveniently out of range; it is all posture and show now – the hierarchy has already been concluded.

Horses live in a hierarchy. They don't really care where they are in the hierarchy, but they must be *in* it. How is this hierarchy settled? In the broadest sense there has to be a lot of posturing and theatre. If horses consistently injured or killed each other, there would be no population to lead or breed. In his thirty- five years of observing wild horses, Dr. Kirkpatrick said he has only witnessed fifteen or twenty knock-down, drag-out fights to the end. So horses understand theatre.

A band of wild horses is moving slowly along the shore of the Atlantic Ocean; they graze peacefully. The flies are bad, so they stay close to the ocean for the breezes and to go into the water if the flies get unbearable. This day, an obstreperous colt is galloping through the herd; he cuts in and out of the mares. He is relentless; it is disturbing. All the other horses are walking or standing, nibbling on tufts of grass. The colt finally runs right past the stallion, still in his own world of obnoxiousness. With the deft precision of a professional hockey player, the stallion steps into the path of the oncoming colt and body-checks him right into the ocean. The colt flies through the air, cartwheeling into the water. He comes up sputtering and coughing, wobbling drunkenly to the shore. The stallion does not even look up. Peace is restored to the group. They continue up the shore, eating. So horses understand force.

21

In the life of a horse, force is used to gain power, and this power allows certain horses to make certain decisions. There is a great deal of posturing, but in the end, there is a role for force. Sometimes the posturing must be backed up.

Two colts are play-fighting. They fall to their knees to protect the important and vulnerable tendons of their lower legs. They fold their legs under their bodies. They swing their strong necks to push the other horse and they try to bite at the hind legs and hocks. A bite on the muscular rump or neck can hurt, but a well-placed bite on the legs can damage a tendon to incapacitate a rival for life. These young colts seem to practise naturally. Horses understand the importance of their teeth and necks. The major cause of death in wild horses will be from complications onset by the loss of their teeth.

What are the components of all the hierarchical posturing? How is this information communicated? What is the language? Xenophon said, 'Anything forced cannot be beautiful', but are there natural legitimate uses for force and, if so, what are they? Aggression, dominance and leadership all involve uses of force, but we know now they are different.

I cannot say how many times people have sent me horses to be trained or retrained, where they have told me they have an 'alpha' mare. What do they really mean? Is the mare just dominant, or is she dominant and aggressive, submissive and aggressive, or insecure and aggressive? Is she a leader of other horses? People often don't understand that all mares, all horses are dominant until they meet another horse and then a decision will be made as to who will submit. Every introduction is, in a sense, a hierarchical evaluation. Remember who you are being introduced to and what perceptive skills they have. If you don't understand the importance of these initial meetings and the language that decodes them, a lot of problems can begin in your relationship with horses.

One of the reasons why horses are so perceptive is their incredible physical attributes. They have almost 360-degree eyesight, and an ability to focus almost simultaneously on the grass they are eating and scan the distance for anything alarming. Horses have complete coats of hair over their bodies and they stand on hard hooves. It's entirely conceivable that they can feel very low frequencies of sound and vibrations from long distances. Their persona is often patronizingly boxed as 'prey animals'. However they are large and powerful and are not often subject to any predation. Dr. Kirkpatrick described to me a scenario in which a wild horse, over a long period of time, stalked a fox – using a subterfuge of grazing to get closer and closer for an attack. 'Horses are not supposed to do this', he said.

Horses' hearing is acute; they can turn their ears independently in different directions, like satellite dishes, to focus in on sounds. Their sense of smell is sophisticated and powerful. They can take in a lot of data. Once they analyse the incoming data, how do they respond, how do they communicate? Horses do use sounds, ranging from the soft murmuring of a mare to her foal, to the ear-shattering screams of stallions that are used for intimidation, or control. Horses also use a rich range of body language. In addition to their acute hearing, the ears of a horse are important indicators of mood; forward and pricked they sense and can indicate alarm, or soften to curiosity. The ears can act independently, flicking back and forth to signal slight agitation. They can be laid back, pinned to the head to display anger or to demonstrate strong agitation which might precede aggression.

The eyes of the horse can squint as if the lids close somewhat to protect these vulnerable organs before the horse goes to fight. They can widen if startled so much that you can see the white sclera as if they are opening to the absolute maximum to allow in as much information as possible.

The lips of the horse can nuzzle softly, reassuring a foal or grooming another horse. They can roll back to display the Flehman gesture; curling they fill their olfactory system with molecules of scent information. Also, of course, the lips can reveal the teeth as in a snarl which might mean, 'These are next if you don't hear me.'

The teeth of the horse are involved at all levels from pleasure to pain. Mares can groom each other peacefully, scratching each other at the withers. They can nip their foals by way of corrections. Stallions may attack each other with mouths wide open, going for blood. (In Portugal I once met a groom with a withered arm that was a result of a stallion grabbing him by the collarbone and lifting him, shaking him like a toy, crushing his shoulder.)

The head of the mare can be used to push a newborn foal gently into a better position for first nursing; four months later, it can bump the same foal out of her food source, telling him to find his own. Small, subtle movements of the head direct other horses; leaders will do little more than look towards another horse to indicate their dominance or encourage movement: 'Now we will get water', or, 'Now we will go to a new feeding area.' Lowering the head and snaking the neck is a sign of agitation and can be coupled with 'suggestions' of movement, herding others or warning them.

The forefeet of the horse can strike and the hind feet can kill; turning the rump toward anything or anyone is a serious statement. The horse can use the body mass to control space on a real and immediate level. In the end, almost all the posturing is aimed at dominating other horses to control their decisions and their movement in space. It's as if whoever controls their space controls their minds. A dominant horse will tell other horses, 'You will allow me to eat first or drink first, step aside.' One stallion tells another, 'I will not allow you to mate with her, stay away.'

In the same way as it can take a lifetime to learn to read poetry, it can take a lifetime to begin to understand the communications of horses, but your life will be richer if you try. If you are going to try to train horses, you will never train any horses well unless they accept your leadership and you earn their respect by making good decisions that they feel and see. You will have to forget about yourself at times and observe and listen to them, especially in the beginning; this knowledge will impact on your success in their letting you handle them.

> Given the obvious 'will to power' (as Friedrich Nietzsche called it) of the human race, the enormous energy put into its expression, the early emergence of hierarchies among children, and the childlike devastation of grown men who tumble from the top, I'm puzzled by the taboo with which our society surrounds this issue. Most psychology textbooks do not even mention power and dominance, except in relation to abusive relationships. Everyone seems in denial.[2]
>
> F. de Waal

[2] F. de Waal, *The Best American Science Writing 2006*, Harper Perennial, 2006.

The initial encounters with particular horses are important and charged with power. It is fairly obvious that if a horse tries to bite or kick you, it's a serious statement that has to be dealt with firmly. However, there are usually many more subtle statements that the horse makes before things ever get that far. There have probably been a multitude of postures that someone has missed. Young horses being broken in will push with their heads and necks; they can get rude when given treats. They can lean into or push against the person grooming them or putting the bridle on. They can refuse to pick up their feet for care. They rush past an object they fear and run into the handler. Every day in the handling of horses there are hundreds of incidents that decide who is in control.

If each and every challenge is met with an inflexible ferocity and tyranny, the horse can get nervous and won't trust – and may even learn to hate – the people in command. On the other hand, if all the incidents are met with leniency, they can lead to disrespect and undisciplined states of instant gratification; the horse will be rude, and have no patience – and you will be held accountable. It would be impossible to list all the potential responses to all the potential incidents that could arise. I think there are some broader systems that can help in the training and handling of horses.

'In all living creatures, from snails to people knowledge of space is central to behavior', as John O'Keefe notes, 'Space plays a role in all our behavior. We live in it, move through it, explore it, defend it.' [3]

In the general treatment of, and communication with horses,

[3] John O'Keefe, quoted in E.Kandel, *In Search of Memory*, W.W. Norton & Company, 2006.

don't underestimate any spatial encounter. Every action and reaction when you are within a certain distance from a horse means something. Especially in the beginning, until you really know what a horse means, you have to create an atmosphere where, as leader, you can control the space; the horse must concede to you. This will be reinforced with the initial longe lessons and in-hand work; on the simplest level, the horse should never turn his rump towards you. In classical training, these psychological matters are constantly addressed, but there is a whole additional plane of physical requirements concerning bend, poll position, etc., which are the building blocks of future collection. Yet the work in the stable is also important: the wrong management in the stable can undo the greatest trainer's work in the riding school.

Does a horse push a person because that horse has always been dominant in nature? Handled correctly, such horses can be fearless – in practical riding situations it might mean that these horses won't shy. Does a horse push a human because that horse is aggressive? If so, is the aggression masking insecurities because the horse is kept constantly enclosed, and like a fear-biting dog, becomes untrustworthy and unstable and angry? Or is the aggression more genetic, as when most of a horse's family line is noted for bad disposition. Dissimilar histories will require dissimilar responses.

When you look for a partner, look for a horse with a good mind and work ethic. He should be neither too bold nor too sensitive. If you want to learn collection, look for someone to work with, not someone to rescue.

In physical terms, look for a well-balanced horse; a lot of balance is natural. You will see it in families. Watch the horse move at freedom – does he do flying changes naturally, or does he counter-canter or cross-canter on the tightest of circles. If the horse is startled, does he spread his forefeet out and duck and stop, or does he step under behind and mock-levade? Watch the hind end: great hock action which bicycles out behind is useless. If you aren't sure of these things, get a professional to help you.

I have been asked a hundred times how it is that obviously bad riding will seem to get amazing performances out of horses. In our stable we don't like it when horses kick the walls, anticipating feeding. So my manager and I came up with a simple solution. If any horse kicks the wall or is unruly before feeding, his feed gets set down outside the stable in plain sight but unreachable; all the other horses are fed. It is amazing how quickly, without any prompting, such horses will learn how to get us to put that feed inside their stable. The horse teaches himself to stop kicking. To me, this is nothing short of the thinking that leads to tool use. The horse learns to move into the middle of the stable, away from the door at feeding time, and the feed comes in promptly. I realized that bad riders essentially do the same thing. The create situations where a frustrated horse goes through the apparently illogical or inappropriate commands and finally gives a response the rider wants, after offering all sorts of choices. It is the opposite of what these riders think: that they understood the horse and they taught the horse. In reality, the horse has understood the rider, illogical signals or not, and has come up with the response the rider wants.

As long as bad riders are somewhat consistent and the training system uses sound biomechanics, even if they are wrong, horses will often figure out what they want over a period of time. Horses will find their way around the illogical blocks. However, if riders are consistent and logical, and give correct aids, the horses learn much faster and are much happier. The classical riding system is such a system. It has evolved over hundreds of years to take into account the psychology of the horse and the biomechanics.

Let me give you an example of two systems of training. A horse and a rider approach a strange object off to their right. The horse is reticent and begins to try to turn away. The rider has been told to lean over to the right and kick the hindquarters to the left. The horse starts to spin on the forehand, the hind legs step over each other, disengaging. After a while the rider stops, and presses the horse forward again. If the horse wants to avoid the unpleasantness, he goes on. The horse has figured out what the rider wants and, to avoid the negative incentives, has conceded. The lesson is, 'Listen to me or you get a negative experience.'

The classical rider feels the horse get tentative about an object off to the right. He immediately uses his left leg and left rein to put the horse into a shoulder-in position. The rider's weight stays above the centre of the horse, but pushes slightly towards the direction they need to go. The hind legs are not disengaged to break up the power train, but are encouraged to step up under the mass and carry and push the shoulders. The outside (right) rein forms a barrier so the horse is channelled into a kind of chute. They pass the object with some tension, but since both horse and rider are looking slightly away from the object, the horse feels there is a way out. Horses ridden in this way are not allowed to investigate everything that seems strange: they are taught to trust the leadership of the rider, and the rider must never ask the horse to do something that might cause him harm. Psychologically, the rider adds another layer of trust once the horse passes the object and nothing happens, the association of fear and displeasure is thus weak and, over time, the problem subsides. In addition to the psychological work, the rider is also gymnastically preparing the horse's body for future work to be symmetrical and balanced. The forehand is unencumbered, so it is easier for the rider to control it. None of this is an accident, but part of a complete system of carefully worked strategies to train the mind and body of the horse. Through an increasingly complicated series of exercises that resemble the training in human ballet, the horse is also trained for performance at a high level, not just to go past an obstacle.

To be successful with horses you need to be consistent, but also to have a physically logical, sound biomechanical system of training, or else you will confuse horses and you can develop behaviours and habits which will preclude you from advancing beyond a certain modest level.

Try to establish a peaceful training stable; don't be disruptive yourself and don't allow others to poison the atmosphere. Horses must have turnout and be able to socialize. They cannot maintain a healthy outlook locked in small stables for twenty-four hours a day. That kind of care is prehistoric. Leave room for different styles; creativity needs space in which to develop, but try not to reinvent the wheel: be aware of the work of your predecessors.

When you have to use force, be prompt and use the least amount of force necessary to change the behaviour – *but change the behaviour!* Try always to leave the horse with a choice and some dignity. Don't corner him. Master posturing, but be prepared to back it up.

Horses are very spatial, as are we. Hold on to your real estate; maintain boundaries. Boundaries are not limiting, they make things fair. Boundaries will define your role as leader; correctly set boundaries will define you as a fair leader. Observe your horses closely, learn their language. Horses need order, and we know that when order is maintained, they feel secure and will thrive instead of being nervous, unsure where they belong, always jockeying for position. I think horses fight some boundaries and are unstable not because they seek a higher position in a hierarchy, but because the hierarchy is unstable and unsteady from day to day. They can't see where the limits are, so they look for them by testing.

Red flags should go up on any encroachment. If you have to back up your decision, be ready to die for it, as horses are masters at bluffing. They recognize it in themselves and others. If they feel it won't be backed up there will be no end to the manipulation. No one ever said the weak will inherit the earth – the biblical phrase was the 'meek' not the 'weak'. Weakness has a way of being displaced. Weak individuals transpose weakness onto individuals weaker than themselves, continuing the chain.

Never be afraid of strength; you can negotiate with strength. Strong animals are secure. If you can't negotiate or compromise you have probably misinterpreted strength for aggression. If that is the case you must go back to holding on to your real estate.

In the end, if you don't find yourself admiring whoever you must lead, or if you think there is a difference between service and leadership, you will be deposed. Your training will be over.

To be part of the life of horses is a reward in itself; to be around them, to take care of them. To learn their language so you can listen to them is beautiful. For a lot of people, this is enough. Yet riding goes beyond this nearness, and collection goes beyond riding. In the practice of collection you and your horse have a chance to merge into something which for a long time in man's history was considered myth.

CHAPTER 3

The Art of Collection in Life and Riding

In 2003, for the first time in the history of riding, the forces and biomechanics of a horse and rider executing the levade (a controlled, balanced rear onto the hind legs of a horse) were measured and described at the McPhail Center in Lansing, Michigan. The McPhail Center is a state-of-the-art biomechanical laboratory for sport horses. It was founded with the foresight and generosity of Mary Anne McPhail, a dressage aficionado, and her husband Walter. Dr. Hilary Clayton chairs the department within the Veterinary College on the campus of Michigan State University. I was the rider in the experiment and my Thoroughbred horse, St. Graal, was my partner. This event was significant. I am recounting it not out of pride, but to explain a motivation generated by an almost opposite emotion of questioning and desperation.

The practice of dressage was being turned on its head, literally. There had been times of upheaval before in the history of dressage, but this was my time and I couldn't go to a comfortable library and read about how it all turned out. No one knew what the outcome would be. It was time to participate.

Some competition dressage riders in particular were promoting systems and theories of training that were in complete contradiction to the classic theory of collection. Riders were forcibly pulling and holding their horses' heads to their chests in complete subjugation, often trying to justify this control with an explanation that this 'stretching' was good for the horse, and horses liked it. There was already good evidence that even mild lowering of the horse's head and neck would shift the weight more to the forehand.[4] It did not seem to matter that this new system contradicted some of the oldest dressage advice – the Duke of Newcastle wrote (1658), 'The whole object of the manège horse is to put the horse upon the haunches' – or that it contradicted current science. Psychologically, this approach is one of unprovoked, unrelenting aggression towards the horse. We have seen that horses' necks are extremely important to them; they understand how to use their necks in settling hierarchical disputes among themselves, but never with this relentlessness. A dispute is settled and then it is over.

There have always been extremes in riding, but rarely have they attained such a strong hold of centre stage. Owing to a strange chain of events and politics, major organizations and judges in competitions found themselves in a position of rewarding the proponents of this extreme on-the-forehand training. If this seems inexplicable, there are countless examples of where, both in corporations and countries, certain powerful groups have become filled with arrogance and hubris. Such groups hold on to positions almost as a matter of pride, even when there

---

[4] H. Clayton, 'The mysteries of collection', *USDF Connection,* July 2003.

is insurmountable evidence against their philosophies and practices. In the context of dressage, the absurdity of this situation came, for me, when some people in power who should have served as guardians defended this abuse with scientific language, often stating that this system had no provable negative effects on a horse when practised by experts. Scientists and artists seemed to be forgetting what they each were supposed to do. The reason why you can't pull a horse's head down to his knees and hold it there is not only because the current science approves or disapproves. The reason why you can't pull a horse's head down to his knees and hold it there day after day, hour after hour, is the same reason why you can't pull a man's head down to his knees and hold it there. The reason is that it is demeaning to the dignity of the horse or man. It is an ethical, philosophical problem, as well as a scientific one. Even in the handling of prisoners of war there are conventions of dignity. When you act this way toward a horse with this unprovoked, irrational and unrelenting constant aggression, you demean everything: the horse, nature, yourself, the art and the observer. In the wild, no horses would accept this demonic control. Leaders lead because they prove they have the capacity to lead, and they are good at it; the whole herd has a better life. If the leaders choose badly, as we have seen, they will be replaced.

For me, even looking beyond the extremists, the demeanour of the times was crystallized by a relatively short statement written by Dr. Hilary Clayton Dr. Clayton has, for years, been working tirelessly with others to establish a baseline of understanding of how horses move and what affects them. She has conducted many experiments to prove and disprove sometimes-accepted conjecture. In this case, Dr. Clayton had been measuring and analysing some top competition dressage horses. When the data was complete she said:

> In many top dressage horses, the weight does not shift significantly from the front to the hind limbs as the horse becomes more collected. However, a few horses do show a marked weight shift, and seem to be the horses that are particularly well balanced. Therefore, balance may indeed be related to the horse's ability to carry more weight on the hindquarters, but the absence of this ability does not preclude a horse from competing successfully at the highest levels of competition.[5]

I believed that there was no scientific 'editing' in these comments – she had simply described what was happening. That a horse could be successful in dressage when on the forehand – balanced to the front – meant either that someone had redefined collection, or that someone was ignoring the body of master work dressage was based upon.

This new kind of dressage was the antithesis of any previous descriptions and ideas about collection. Since collection had always been the heart and soul of dressage, I wondered if there was something inherent in competitive dressage that was allowing or even pushing an evolution away from classical principles to a different dressage, with different objectives, different concepts. Was it possible that the traditional classical concepts of collection were faulty from the beginning and that this was now being revealed by the new sophisticated

[5] H. Clayton, 'What is biomechanics?', *The American Hanoverian Magazine*, Fall 1999.

tools of science? I realized no one as yet had definitive proof.

The reason why collection has been the heart and soul of dressage is that it is a method that prepares a horse and rider to do airs above the ground. These airs are the culmination of high-school riding; they are jumps or gestures of balance off the powerful hind legs of the horse. Their evolution possibly began as war movements. Riders, in theory, might have used certain rears, kicks, jumps and spins to free themselves from the pressures of an enemy. However, there are writings from the past that cause us to question the extent to which this was so. The Duke of Newcastle (1592–1676), who had battlefield experience, said: 'Even the best horsemen find it difficult to make the horse do "airs" at any time, and after three days campaigning they will not go in "airs", even if you would have them.' Thomas Blundeville, writing earlier, in the reign of Elizabeth I, said of the airs: '. . . it is quite sufficient if in the entire royal stables there should be two or three horses capable of these movements', which doesn't suggest they were necessary requisites of warhorses. They also have a deeper source, as most of them will occur in rougher forms when horses play or exhibit courtship displays, etc., so they came from a natural wellspring. They can be exotic, but they are natural. It was important to the master horsemen that they tried to enhance nature, but not to indulge in artificiality as homage to nature.

Irrespective of any practical use in fighting, these movements quickly became symbolized and practised for their beauty, grace, power and excitement. They became stylized and were given specific names and requirements which separated them from random explosions of an agitated or excited horse. The mastery was in learning to control this exquisite power. A horse had to be trained to jump and to rear safely, on command,

and so collection was born. It became a process whereby a horse using specific balletic exercises develops the strength, elasticity and control to execute the airs safely. Collection has some serious physical demands and objectives for both horse and rider. It also has very important psychological elements.

Collection became understood as a centring of focus for the rider and horse. The rider had to be able to learn how to keep disciplined and focused in the midst of dangerous training manoeuvres day after day. In order to have any chance of learning how to train a horse to collect, riders had to be able to collect themselves first.

Collection is to mentally and physically gather yourself to your core. It is a preparation to enter 'flow'.

In his book *Emotional Intelligence,* Daniel Goleman states:

Flow is a state of self forgetfulness, the opposite of rumination and worry... Because flow feels so good, it is intrinsically rewarding... Instead of being lost in nervous preoccupation, people in flow are so absorbed in the task at hand that they lose all self-consciousness, dropping the small preoccupations – health, bills, even doing well – of daily life. In this sense moments of flow are egoless. Paradoxically, people in flow exhibit a masterly control of what they are doing, their responses perfectly attuned to the changing demands of the task. And although people perform at their peak while in flow, they are unconcerned with how they are doing, with thought of success of failure – the sheer pleasure of the act itself is what motivates them. [6]

[6] D. Goleman, *Emotional Intelligence*, Bantam Books, 1995.

It has also been observed that: 'When people are engaged in activities that effortlessly capture and hold their attention, their brain "quiets down" in the sense that there is a lessening of cortical arousal.'[7]

When in a state of flow, skills are well rehearsed and neural circuits at their most efficient. The individual's repetitive training impresses a complete muscular or mental memory of the task at hand. Outside forces seem to be neutralized, biochemicals and hormones seem to be administered at the rate of your choosing. The artist is free of the technique you have practised for so long.

'Painters must want to paint above all else. If the artist in front of the canvas begins to wonder how much he will sell it for, or what the critics will think of it, he won't be able to pursue original avenues. Creative achievements depend on single-minded immersion.'[8] Today, too many riders are controlled by outside forces; the attention is always being drawn out of them, towards a championship, toward celebrity, toward a prize always further and further from themselves.

Collection was a process that was very similar for the horse. The horse had to gather himself for a supreme physical effort, but still had to accept the discipline of control. Once horses know a movement they can get anxious in anticipation. One of the classical requirements is that all high-school jumps must be preceded by piaffe or terre-à-terre. The piaffe is a modified, highly collected trot in which the horse hardly moves forward

[7] J. Hamilton et al., 'Intrinsic enjoyment and boredom coping scales: validation with personality, evoked potential and attention measures', *Personality and Individual Differences* 5,2, 1984.
[8] Dr. Csikszentmihalyi, interview by D. Goleman, *The New York Times*, arch 22, 1992.

but is gathering himself in a continuous motion, waiting for the proper signal to leap. It stores power and balances the horse. The terre-à-terre is a canter-based preparation. Here, the horse canters in a shorter and shorter stride, jumping front to back, the two hind legs pushing onto two forelegs and back, coiling more and more on the hind legs, again waiting for the rider to make sure everything is right before the jump.

The main reason for these requirements is that, if the horse leaps without the proper set-up, this can be very dangerous for both horse and rider. The horse could fall over backwards and crush the rider. If the horse pushes off from one leg, a misstep could result in a career-ending injury. If the trainer does not build the poise into the horse, the horse might just bolt through the bridle and nothing could stop him. The horse must be taught how to build up power to repeat the airs safely, otherwise there is no art, but undisciplined, unrepeatable movement and, too often, injurious accidents.

In the late sixteenth century, Spanish troops were on Italian soil, and with them they had brought their Iberian horses. These were compact horses with fast reflexes and good minds. It was as if the Spanish horse met the forces of the Renaissance and the great écuyers had a vehicle with which to fully express and explore their equestrian art. The Italian trainer Pignatelli had a school to which noblemen came from all over Europe. The students were a 'Who's Who' of the riders who shaped what I would call modern dressage.

One of Pignatelli's students, Antoine de Pluvinel, went on to serve four French kings as the master of the master horsemen. De Pluvinel was highly aware of the potential for dressage to enlighten and teach self-control. A famous book of his is essentially a dialogue with the young king of France.[9] In this book, while explaining the art, de Pluvinel pleads for the funding for more riding academies. Here, they could continue to teach 'virtue', whereby they could curb the impetuousness of France's youths, who were continually obsessed with deadly duels; academies where they could produce classical men who could think clearly under pressure. De Pluvinel saw that riders had to learn great self-control in order to marshal and command the forces of a powerful, excited horse. A young rider had to stand next to an excited young stallion, muscles quivering in anticipation, and hold fast when the first jumps went off crooked and the horse, perhaps 10 feet (3 m) above him, could come down on top of him. Riders had to learn to watch closely the feet of the young horse: if the first wild, untrained kicks were mistimed, they had the potential to kill or maim a man. De Pluvinel knew that false bravado would be disastrous. The training had to be built upon discipline and skill. Riders trained for years, intellectually and emotionally. Gratification was often delayed or withheld. There was often only a promise that, one day, you would be able to do it. It took great faith in the instructor and it took passion to overcome the daily struggle. Patience, courage and respect were all inevitable outcomes.

In the process, students and teachers also revealed themselves. For some, the hard work was self-fulfilling; others needed constant reinforcement. In the process, instructors' motivations would be revealed: some were educators; some were absorbed in self-promotion.

De Pluvinel knew all this as a practical matter. He wanted

[9] A. de Pluvinel, *The Maneige Royal*, translated into English and with an Introduction by Hilda Nelson, J.A. Allen & Co Ltd, 1989.

teachers to receive good salaries to give them some security so as to limit competition between them. In the end, however, I am sure that he knew much of this was beyond his control. He must have made some peace between the politics and the process. For decades, he stood near the centre of the most political situations, pursuing an apolitical endeavour. I think de Pluvinel realized that all he could do was teach collection, and collection could train a mind and body, and a trained mind could choose better than a wild mind or an indoctrinated mind.

You *can* collect when nothing is going to happen and it has therapeutic value like meditative practices. In my mind, however, you *must* collect when something exciting or dangerous is imminent, in order to stay alive.

I believe this is what de Pluvinel wanted his students to learn. I believe it is what we need to know, and it is one of the greatest gifts riding can give.

I think de Pluvinel understood that the security of a society was inextricably linked to the security of the individual… In the late eighteenth century, the French monarchy was destroyed in a matter of days. Those who learned to think politically died politically. Those who had learned collection kept dressage alive. Or was it, dressage kept them alive?

CHAPTER 4

The Levade

A family goes on vacation somewhere in western America. One day they have lunch at an inexpensive restaurant, outside on the wooden deck that surrounds the building. There are some plywood figures with holes cut out at the face: a well-proportioned dancing girl, garters showing, her dress hiked up, breasts full and half out of the propped-up top; a cowboy, tall, slim, reserved, and maybe even a period dog. The wife takes a picture of her husband placing his head where the cowboy's face should be, and now she has his cowboy image as a permanent portrait. The husband takes a fantasy photo of his wife as a sexy saloon girl.

In the eighteenth century, there was a kind of analogous situation, only it was a lot more serious and a lot more expensive. The author W. Liedtke has explained how various members of royal dynasties would have official portraits made, and many times the 'plywood cut-out' of choice was to be painted with the subject of the portrait on a horse performing the levade, so you see painting after painting of various monarchs and other people of very high social status in very similar poses.[10]

If you wanted to show your status, you had to pick a symbol that even the most plebeian person would understand. A horse in levade was it. Even though the other airs were often greater acrobatic feats and the poser didn't actually have to ride the movement anyway, the levade was 'the' symbol of elite, powerful, phenomenal control, balance and class. If even just half of the subliminal connections would attach to the monarch of the day, the painting would be a success. It was masterful image-making before press and publicists and advertising campaigns – in case anyone thinks that is a new phenomenon.

To me, the interesting thing is how universal the consciousness is, even among non-horsemen, of the pre-eminence of the image of levade. Not only are there countless paintings of it – there are little porcelain pieces for individual shelves in individual houses, and great bronzes in city parks and squares. It's everywhere, even in places where there are no more horses. It is an icon representing sustained power, balance, restraint, and taste: no one has to be beaten over the head with statements; it's obvious.

When I began to study and train the airs above the ground, I had to make a choice. I was competing my horses at Grand Prix. I wondered whether, if I began teaching the levade, would I risk grounding my piaffe?

Little did I realize how important this question was and what its ramifications were for my learning about dressage. What if I collected too much in the piaffe during the middle of a test and the horse reared? No judge or observer would understand; I was sure it would be viewed as a serious evasion.

---

[10] W. Liedtke, *The Royal Horse and Rider*, Abaris Books, 1989.

In the beginning, at most schools of riding today, everything you will be taught is aimed towards preventing or rectifying the rearing horse. All my life, up until this point, in jumping, eventing and dressage, I had been taught that to rear is bad. If it happens, you might let go of the reins, usually leaning forward, or you jump off; you get angry with your horse because it is a most dangerous evasion. In a normal fall off a horse, you can get a broken arm or leg, but if a horse comes over on top of you, the full weight will divide the rider and the horse risks striking the back of his head into the ground with enough force to cause death.

Twenty years ago, I wrote about how my own bad riding created a rearing horse and how the horse and I were luckily spared any serious injury. Since then, however, like the surfers of Chapter 1, I had been self-sculpting. I became a different rider – although I work on the same personality every day. I was ready to work with the airs. What makes uncontrolled rearing so dangerous is what makes controlled rearing so exciting. Fear, risk and adrenalin amplify your curiosity, your questions, and heighten your experiences. (Although any fool can heighten experience, only with practice can you do it with regularity and control.) For me, it was time to go beyond Grand Prix.

CHAPTER 5

Science – Measuring Collection

The experiment was to measure the forces and describe the biomechanics of the transition from piaffe to levade. We already knew that the forelegs were being used to generate a certain amount of lift in the piaffe. Even though Dr. Clayton had said the well-balanced horses do shift their weight to the rear, I felt that it could be argued that using the forelegs to collect was, in fact, normal and it could validate those rider/trainers who were executing piaffes overburdened on the forehand, and were nevertheless successful in competition. Stopping the measuring at the piaffe would never answer or describe collection with any finality. We had to pass the piaffe and collect data on the ultimate dressage movements: the airs. If we could measure the set-up of the levade out of the piaffe we could see how the horse was doing this. If the forelegs pushed the forehand up, it would question the great preponderance of classical literature. If the forehand was pulled up by the muscles of the back, abdomen and hindquarters, it could validate 300-year-old, as yet unproven theories.

I couldn't help but think back thirty years to a discussion I had with the great old horseman Vladimir Littauer. Littauer had written that jumping horses approaching a fence ricocheted or rebounded off their forelegs to set up for the fence, and that this force was very important. To that end, as I remember, he had developed a teaching method to facilitate the process in order to get maximum recoil. I had friends in the hunter-jumper discipline who were developing a style of riding to fences that aimed to deliberately encourage the horse to lean on the forehand. The result of this technique was that horses, feeling 'buried' in front of the fence, would pull their forehands up sharply. It was this added snap that these riders loved to see, and this look of the front end became their obsession, even though it could only work if the fences weren't too high. It was likely that there was a rebounding force off the forelegs; however, to me, any riding theory had to place the most importance on the collecting over the hind legs. My theory was that, instead of throwing the reins away, you had to use them and their contact (albeit lightly) to connect the horse on the approach, to help the horse bascule and thus lift the forehand up. I thought I could prove it to Littauer when I photographed one of my horses repeatedly jumping a 3-foot (0.9 m) fence from a dead standstill. My feeling was that, in this situation, there could be little or no upward thrust from the forelegs. The greatest amount of work was being done by the sinking and coiling under of the hind legs, which was clearly visible from the photographs, and which I measured. In my eyes, the pictures were decisive. As I recall, my best argument wouldn't sway him. Later, I met Dr. George Pratt of MIT, one of the pioneers in equine biomechanics. He had used force plates to measure the forces on horses' legs and feet unequivocally. I talked to him about doing an experiment to measure the forces on a jumping horse's feet to settle the debate. Although we never got to do the experiment, he did some mathematical calculations which proved that the hind end did, of course, do the lion's share of lifting and propulsion.

I was using dressage theory to help clarify my understanding of jumping. I never thought that, in an ironic sense, this front-end thinking would actually infiltrate dressage and I would be revisiting this matter. Once again I was back looking to the best scientists of my day to help me understand what was going on.

The heart of the McPhail Center is a beautiful indoor riding arena with vaulting arched wooden rafters. On one side of the long wall there is a rubber runway. A rider can ride right out of the sand onto the runway, which is exactly the same height. Halfway up the long wall is an alcove set back from the runway. In the spacious recessed area the high-speed cameras are positioned, computers are arranged, and the team can observe. The force plate is on the rubber runway, concealed under the floor directly in front of the cameras. As the horse passes, all the data is gathered. The team analyses it and, in due time, they publish their findings.

It was a thirteen-hour drive from my farm to the Michigan State University. St. Graal was not a great traveller and didn't like to drink, so we stopped often, pulled grass from along the highway to keep him happy and fed him lots of carrots. In order to make the most of the trip, the plan was that I would do the experiment, give a clinic and do an evening demonstration ride as a fundraiser for the McPhail Center. It was going to be a long weekend.

Of course, the experiment was the foremost thing on my

mind. When we arrived there, even though I had participated in experiments before, I seemed to have forgotten how small the force plate was: maybe 18x36 in (45x90 cm). I wasn't sure how I was going to be able to land on it with St. Graal's footfalls.

First, we were fitted with reflective markers – both horse and rider had these shiny little 'golf balls' glued on. These markers were placed on all significant joints and areas of movement. Working together, the cameras and computers would digitalize the form of the moving horse and rider and reduce it to a magical stick figure, which could be measured, rotated, viewed from above and below, thereby giving it a life of its own. These were some of the state-of-the-art software systems that people were using in popular films. Six scientists stood by patiently as the markers were glued on, and as the battery pack I carried was tested. Computers were checked and rechecked.

I had come to realize that the speed of science is somewhat illusionary; we see advances in computers and science almost overnight, but we don't realize the endless human hours spent tediously setting up machines, or see the countless failed batteries and broken wires. Six Doctors and six hours, just to film a small piece of riding – and that's just to collect some data; it doesn't include analysis. All the people there were very professional, patient and polite in spite of work that must get immensely frustrating at times.

Finally, the cameras were turned on; the runway was like a movie set. First, I made a whole series of practice runs over the plate in piaffe to get a feel for the task. It seemed easy enough, except that under the force plate the floor was hollow. When St. Graal stepped on it the first time is sounded different from the solid footing, like a drum. He became suspicious. We would be coming directly towards it in a perfectly straight piaffe and then, knowing exactly where it was, like a dancer gracefully avoiding a puddle, he deftly changed the angle of his leg for one or two steps and deliberately missed the plate, while continuing in a perfectly straight line.

After a few more passes, St. Graal settled and we hit the mark again and again. I could hear the computer make a satisfying loud beep when we got a good hit.

It was time to try the levade. I had to bring St. Graal in piaffe over the plate, which was then behind me. I could hear the beeps as he stepped in a rhythm on the plate then, when I felt it was right, I collected the piaffe more and more until his forehand lifted from the ground and we balanced over his hind legs. We had all realized the force plate was too narrow to accommodate both hind legs. When St. Graal settled back he had to widen his stance; later the amazing analysis would show how subtly he rocked slightly from one hind foot to the other to find his balance.

Dr. Clayton was encouraging. She explained that, if we could get one leg on the plate, we could extrapolate the other: it should be half the force. So we tried piaffe, piaffe, settle back, no beep – we missed. Again, again, the lights seemed hotter and hotter. St. Graal was sweating, but I knew he wouldn't quit.

Now, more than ever before, I had first-hand insight into the advice of the masters. The jumps must come out of a secure piaffe, otherwise you will lose control and they will just be tricks. When you have to repeat airs like this, the horse anticipates naturally. The classical trainer has built in the control by mastering piaffe so that even the excited horse waits. St. Graal was magnificent; he let me try again and again. I thought to myself, the theory works – although I don't think they had this many repetitions in mind.

What we were doing was not so much two 'tricks' – a piaffe and a levade – but showing that they were nothing more than a continuation of one process: 'collection'. The feeling was straining and exhilarating at the same time. Finally, we had enough good hits. St. Graal's neck and hind legs were white with sweat. I hoped it was enough; I knew that there was nothing more either of us could do.

The next night was the demonstration. St. Graal felt wonderful; he could sometimes be nervous, but he seemed to love this crowd. I have to admit that we had done so many levades the day before I was afraid he might be too keen, so I sort of tricked him by changing the choreography slightly; I put the piaffe and levade in a different place, and kept him from anticipating. We demonstrated all the Grand Prix movements, albeit conservatively, plus levade and pesade.

In the following weeks, Dr. Clayton and her team analysed the data and eventually published the results.[11] *The force on St. Graal's forelegs did not increase as he went from piaffe to levade. Instead, the muscles of the hindquarters, abdomen and back pulled his front end up and back over his hind legs.* St. Graal had collected himself. Of all the levades we attempted that day, the shortest was 0.8 seconds in duration, and the longest was 2.5 seconds. To give you a reference point, a horse jumping a 5 ft (1.5 m) fence will be in the air for half a second from take-off to landing. Thus even the shortest levade was balanced longer than all the air time

[11] H. Clayton, 'Learning about the levade', *USDF Connection*, October 2003.

of a 5 ft (1.5 m) jump, and in the longest levade St. Graal had balanced over his hind legs five times longer than the air time of such a jump. The levade is an incredible feat of strength and balance. It deserves its reputation.

Afterwards, my feelings were strange. There was a sense of relief that we had a definitive proof and description of the classicists' idea of collection. At the same time, I had even more reverence for my predecessors who invented these movements and mastered them, and believed in them without definitive proofs. I felt very lucky to have my question answered this time, but I knew that whatever you want to do, there may not be enough science to answer your questions. There will, however, always be enough art to propose them. It will be the artists who propose them.

At the beginning of this chapter I asked if there was something in competitive dressage that was contributing to the loss of collection, and even to a loss of understanding of the ideas of collection. If collection was always the heart and soul of dressage, logically a loss of understanding of collection would mean a loss of the idea of what dressage really was.

With more and more study, I began to believe that competitive dressage had unwittingly set in motion a series of self-limits by eliminating the airs above the ground, which are the ultimate proof of collection. Imagine if a school of ballet evolved that way: a ballet that never left the floor, no jumps. What would it look like; what dancers would it favour? It's not hard to see, with an obsession on movement across the ground, how these ground-bound aberrations like rollkur and piaffe on the forehand could develop. The trend was to differentiate performances not by mastery of collection, but by the size and speed of movement. Quality of movement is too subjective. Quantifying movement bigger or faster would be easier to score. There was one small problem – this new riding wasn't dressage as it has been evolving for 2,000 years.

The obvious next question for me was: could this situation be fixed so future generations of riders wouldn't lose this art? Would adding jumps to competition automatically fix this problem, or did the execution of the exercises that themselves led to the airs have to be performed a certain way? Did some people have to rethink their objectives in the classical exercises?

CHAPTER 6

Riding Inside the System – 'A Model for Collection'

As we have seen, a great deal of communication between horses is done with their heads and necks. Horses control other horses with gestures and/or direct contact with their teeth, muzzles, ears, heads and necks. They are thus familiar with control in these areas.

The earliest horsemen realized that whoever controls the head and neck of the horse controls the horse. Therefore, one of their first inventions was the bit. This became a central theme in riding that has lasted to the present day. In most horse-human activities and equestrian sports, the greatest attention is on controlling the mouth and neck of the horse. The range of equipment that is employed in trying to do this speaks for itself: martingales, draw reins, sliding reins, bitting rigs and every imaginable bit and hackamore – even some devices and techniques that are better not imagined.

History, of course, repeats itself; in the current climate the battle around the practice of rollkur is a mirror of the vitriolic argument highlighted by Seeger's and Steinbrecht's caustic comments on the neck and jaw manipulations of Baucher in the mid-nineteenth century. The obsession repeats itself, as someone will always be looking for a shortcut around the slow, progressive work of learning collection.

Most of the obsessions rooted in trying to control the horse with a bit come from a simple physical problem. The horse has a far greater mass than the horseman. A human can walk up to a soccer ball and kick it and, because of the human's superior inertia, the ball moves. By applying force, the human displaces the ball because it has less inertia.[12] However there is no way a human being can, by kicking a horse, physically apply enough force to displace the horse's inertia. (In general, whether we are talking about mechanics for engineering and physics, or biomechanical forces on bodies or systems, they can be separated as external or internal. In most riding, because of the problem of the horse's greater inertia, the forces that the rider exerts on the horse are external to the system of the horse.) Accepting this simple fact gives birth to a whole training programme that at its best can evolve into an art form and at its worst degenerates into sadism.

In the early stages of training or controlling the horse, the horse must initially move himself. The rider could never physically move a horse who is standing still in a stable position, no matter what gyrations they did on top of the horse. (If you have ever tried to train a horse to jump into water when the horse didn't want to, you know how stable horses can become

[12] H. Clayton, 'The dynamic horse', *Sport Horse Publications*, Fall 1999.

on the edge of the bank.) The human can devise strong incentives for the horse to move – whether rewards or punishments – but when the horse is in a stable, balanced form, he has a superior physical advantage.

So, in the early stages of training we rely on signals, cues and associations that the horse recognizes and differentiates between. Once in motion, good rider posture will give the rider much more power by effectively using leverage in various forms, but still the signals from the rider will be external, that is from outside the system of the horse. There really is no reason why the horse couldn't learn to do all ridden tasks from the voice or sound alone, with no touching. This would not be 'riding', but it would be more humane than some bad riding which is so confusing that it is amazing horses can figure it out.

As a horse collects, a curious phenomenon begins to occur. The horse becomes more manoeuvrable but is less stable. In the levade, the horse is quite beautifully balanced but quite unstable – easy to affect, easy to upset with either good or bad riding. The rider's influences and forces change from external suggestions outside the system of the horse to internal forces within the new system of horse and rider. The rider and horse become one system; one body. The clichés about becoming one with your horse actually have physical merit as you enter into the world of collection.

Many riders have actually been in this place, usually when they have caused an accident. When they were leaning the wrong way when a horse tripped, or when a horse slipped on some bad footing. Very few riders go to this place on purpose. Yet this is the place where the cliché to be one with your horse becomes a biomechanical reality; where science and art meet.

So much of the classical dressage literature is dedicated to getting the rider to want to leave the utilitarian role of performing tricks, where cues and responses can be done from outside the system and where the quality of your riding isn't important, and to enter instead into the system of balance and become an active and responsible partner in all kinds of movements.

Constant advice like 'don't ride the bridle', 'stop twisting the neck', 'quiet hands', 'ride the hind end', all aims to help the rider toward artistic riding and away from the centuries of obsession with head and neck controls; to coax the rider past the issue of dominance and submission. Who will dominate? Who will be submissive? The art of dressage has been to go beyond hand riding to seat riding. The pursuit of collection is the process that can enable this: acknowledging the goal informs the practice. The better the balance and mastery of collection, the more manoeuvrable the horse becomes, and the more responsive to the weight aids. It is obvious in this line of communication that the quality of your riding becomes extremely important. That is why, in the traditional classical riding instruction, many years of effort are necessary to learn the correct position which allows the rider to move the onus of direction towards the seat and weight aids – with the hands and reins into a more auxiliary role. All the exercises in the sitting trot are the same for the rider as the scales are for the musician and class is for the dancer. Unless riders master their own balance and body they will not be able to go to that 'level of dance'. They are destined to stay at a certain level of displays of associative learning and never feel the freefall freedom of a creative process; something happening almost intuitively out of a field of seemingly mundane technique. In this latter world, the rider feels as if their body is directly connected to the horse.

A Model for Collection

THE HIND END

The muscles of the hind end flex and extend the hind legs. This huge piston-like action is controlled by the gluteals, biceps and quadriceps femoris; it is the motor of the horse, and the source of so much of the power. This great motor must be swung forward and brought under the mass of the horse in order to lift it and propel it forwards. Otherwise the hind legs could simply pump up and down, working like mad but to no avail.

A pole vaulter runs towards the jump, gaining kinetic energy. He plants the pole out in front of him. His momentum keeps coming forward; the pole flexes, gathering energy, changing the vaulter's energy into potential energy. The pole then begins to unleash its stored power, sending the vaulter forward and upward.

In the horse's skeleton, the lumbo-sacral joint is the hinge point. It is the only joint in the relatively stationary section of spine from the withers to the pelvis. Perhaps the most important muscles for collection are the iliopsoas and psoas.[13] These muscles work deep inside the horse's body and operate that hinge. With the help of the abdominals, they will lower the pelvis and bring the great motor of the hind legs under the mass

[13] S. Wyche, *The Horse's Muscles in Motion*, Crowood Press, 2002.

and then, when these great legs drive off the ground, the iliopsoas and psoas will again brace so that the lower back and stifles don't get overextended, and end up bearing all of the force, or letting the power escape.

If the pole vaulter's hands slipped off the pole as he was climbing, he would fall flat on his back going nowhere – the pole, now unencumbered, would snap back so fast it might break; the energy is accidentally released too fast. In the horse's system the iliopsoas and psoas keep these kind of things from happening. They are 'the hands on the pole'.

In the simplest sense, the iliopsoas and psoas facilitate the engagement of the hind legs and, if they aren't working, there can't be any engagement. If the rider, whether through faulty position or incorrect training technique, locks this hinge *down* and forces the hind legs out behind by sitting too far back or too heavily, or rides so slowly that there is no engagement, or rides so fast that the horse's hind legs are out too far behind, collection is impossible. Conversely, if the rider (again, by faulty position or technique) locks this hinge *up* by stiffening the horse's loins in a roached, humped-up position, collection will also be impossible. For me, watching a very highly trained dressage horse go from a trot to a good piaffe to a levade is magical. The difficulty is extreme and the core strength and graceful control of this hinge are absolute proof that horse and rider have mastered collection at the highest level; decelerating while tipping the weight backwards is sublime.

THE FRONT END

At the front end of the horse, the brachiocephalicus and omotransversarius, the big throaty muscles on the underside of the neck, pull the foreleg up and forwards.[14] They connect from the shoulder area towards the head. If the neck is not fixed up and forward they will overpower the neck and pull the head down. However, when the neck is fixed in a strong upward arch, when the horse is on the bit (meaning the poll is at the highest point and the face is at or slightly in front of vertical), the forelegs can be lifted.

In riding, the secret here is that the base of neck must be up, starting the great arch. Think of a horse chesting a fence and eating grass on the other side. The base of the neck first must be up to go over the fence, then the horse can stretch out and down. All of a sudden, the horse sees another horse approaching on the other side of the fence: he stays in position but raises his neck like a stallion to meet the other horse. On the underside of the neck, the scalenus and on the topside of the neck, the serratus, contract to take out the dropping curve of the spine and push the base of the neck up and forward, going from an almost ewe-necked position to the beginnings of a crested position. Even though the base of the neck is now up, this is just the start of a collected position. The horse cannot raise the front end or come off the forehand in this position alone. On the topside of the neck, the serratus contracts around the fulcrum of the withers connecting the neck and the first few ribs. The splenius attaches to the head as well as the nuchal ligament system and gives the beautiful crest its shape. When the rider feels this, it seems as though the horse's neck is woven into the back and the horse feels as if 'of one piece'. Even a novice rider could feel how 'throughness' would be possible and where the concept came

---

[14] S. Wyche, *The Horse's Muscles in Motion*, Crowood Press, 2002.

from when feeling this connection. In fact, that is exactly what is happening; the neck and back become solidly connected. It is a platform for bascule.

Finally, when the neck is raised up and out and the poll flexed, the great arch of the nuchal ligament system is tensed and forms a counterbalance for the brachiocephalicus and omotransversarius to pull against. Anyone who has ever hit their nose against the crested neck of a horse while learning to jump knows how this nuchal system can feel as strong as steel.

There are a million logos on tea cups and tee shirts, and thousands of auction photos of horses with their necks up and a foreleg extended, not fully straight out, but with a great, free shoulder and a slight bend at the knee. The forearm is lifted in this graceful, almost soft, way that seems to say: 'See my power, see how easy it is.' We must love this pose of the front end because it is displayed everywhere. It is this pose which exemplifies the balance and counterbalance and the interplay of the powerful neck and the arm.

If we go back to our analogy of the horse chesting a fence and grazing on the other side, we have the base of the neck still up, but the great arch of the topline relaxes and stretches out. Without the great contraction it is almost as if the brachiocephalicus and omotransversarious pull the neck down. This is a posture we use to warm up the horse, or cool down. In a sense it is an antidote to the demands of collection. There are many riders who have become seduced by this feeling; they love the looseness of the topline and they even try to propose theories about how this posture will develop collection. In reality, it's relationship to collection is like one of rest to stress. All physical exercise needs to be followed by periods of rest and sleep to recover. So there is an important *association* between the relaxed looseness of the topline and collection but it is not a *causative* one. These riders have forgotten that it is the antithesis of collection and horses cannot put themselves upon their haunches in this form. Writers as far back as Grisone (in the sixteenth century) noted that the back must be tight and firm to prepare for high collection and jumps. So the serratus, scalenus, splenius, brachiocephalicus, omotransversarious and the nuchal ligament system all are involved in elevating the forehand.

There are no bony attachments from the forelimbs of the horse to the body. The ribcage of the horse hangs in a sling. When the serratus ventralis and pectorals contract they help raise this thoracic sling.[15] The rider can feel as though the withers seem to rise up. These muscles also connect the ribcage area to the forces of the forelimbs. If they were totally loose, the vertical force of the forelegs – the 'ground reaction forces' – could go past the loose thorax, instead of supporting and even helping to lift the forehand at certain points of the stride.

THE MIDDLE

No matter how much the hind end curls under, no matter how perfect the neck position and how perfectly the front end works to elevate the forelegs, you cannot have collection until both ends are connected. Traction and connections of the longissimus, latissimus, psoas, multifidus, spinalis and splenius draw the topline together, but this action must be counterbalanced by the abdominals.

There used to be a wonderful child's toy call a Slinky. It was

---

[15] H. Clayton, 'Components of collection', *Dressage Today*, October 2007.

actually a loosely coiled spring. When it was compressed, just sitting there on a table, it was about the size of a coffee mug, just a silver steel cylinder with no top or bottom. If you picked it up and stretched it out it was loose; you could pull it the length of your arms. When you pulled it apart, like opening the bellows of an accordion, gravity would pull the middle section down between your hands. It would sag, since it had no support in the middle. You can think of the horse's torso as a cylinder connecting the front end to the back. If the rider theoretically stretches the back out far enough, gravity will pull it down in the middle. You might say that the abdominals will hold it up, but they can't because they would need to contract to do that and you have asked them to relax to get maximum stretch and length of the torso.

Now, if the rider only influences contraction on the topline, a similar 'U' shape will become apparent, like when a horse kicks. The contraction of the topside will push the belly down. If we bring our hands closer together with our toy and push the top of the cylinder together, our toy will sag again at the bottom. Albeit, the curve will be stiffer, but it will still sag. If we push the whole thing together again, the top and bottom all the way equally, it reforms a tight cylinder, like a short section of pipe.

The beauty of the cylinder of the horses' torso is the harmonic way the abdominals counterbalance the contraction of the back. When it is done correctly the whole cylinder becomes shorter and stronger; it does not sag or, in our terminology, the back does not hollow out. When riders are not used to feeling collection they get afraid of the tone of this connectivity – they often think it is stiffness creeping in and immediately let the horse out again. But this is not stiffness, this is natural, and it requires a good seat to stay with the shorter oscillations of the back.

Without this tension there could not be 'throughness' because there would not be any connection of the front and hind ends. If we spread our Slinky out and move one hand up or down, it is totally ineffective as a lever as it is too soft, but if we connect it like a solid pipe, leverage is direct. The back becomes the central axis of bascule, where a counterbalance device pivots around that central axis so that the unweighted end rises while the weighted end is allowed to fall.[16] The horse's back connects to the weighted haunches and helps lift the unweighted forehand. Look at any picture of the levade, and see the breadth of the back and abdominals; the horse's belly looks like marble in its tone and expanse.

Today, we use the term very loosely, but core strength is what we are talking about.

When I first stood next to a horse, training the levade in hand, I remember how it was almost frightening to be next to such power. The whole underside of the horse seemed to expand and expand almost to a breaking point. The muscles would quiver; many times the horse would explode towards a courbette. Since you invariably begin to train along an immovable wall, only your courage will help keep the horse channelled in that small corridor of space. An exuberant or disrespectful horse can come right on top of you.

To witness this core strength from so close is thrilling. Then to ride it, is what a dressage rider trains for all their life. Now, you have mastered the sensation of collecting onto the hind legs. You

[16] A.H. Soukhanov (US General Editor), et al., *Encarta World English Dictionary*, St. Martin's Press, 1999.

These are some of the classical exercises which, when practised correctly, build the connection from back to front, lightening the forehand. When the horse is strong enough and balanced enough, the lightening reaches its apex in the levade where there is no weight on the forehand at all.

1. Half-pass

2. Doux passage

3. Piaffe
4. Piaffe

5. Shoulder-in

6. Levade

7. Levade

8. Levade

deliberately go inside the system, partnering with forces well beyond your own personal limitations. Yet, you can't start there, and neither can the horse. You have to start with the classic exercises and they have to be executed in a certain way or they will not enhance collection, and may even preclude it.

A MODEL TO RIDE THE MODEL

There is no doubt that riding has fostered obsession in head control and neck shapes. Systems of riding that weaken the neck or disconnect it at the poll or withers might give the rider temporary control, but they disturb the horse's ability to connect himself along the whole spinal posture. Even slight movement of body parts away from the central balancing posture can disturb the animal's equilibrium – both horse and rider in this case – and make collection impossible.

If a riding system asks the neck to stretch out and/or down, even small changes will inhibit the horse's ability to collect. It's unequivocal that moving the neck this way places the horse more on the forehand, adding more weight to a ratio that is already naturally tipped toward the forelegs.

CHAPTER 7

All Roads Don't Lead to Rome

The arts have a development which comes not only from the individual, but also from a cumulative force, the civilization which precedes us. One cannot do just anything. A talented artist cannot do whatever he pleases. If he only used his gifts, he would not exist. We are the not the master of what we produce. It is imposed upon us.

Matisse

I have noticed that, when most riders or trainers of one school watch another trainer who gives advice that contradicts what they have been saying, a dismissive attitude will surface. If the work they have seen is too good to ignore, they will explain the contradiction by saying that there are many ways to achieve the same results. If they don't understand the work, it will be overruled almost always with some sarcasm. When you feel this way as a trainer, you have to analyse your immediate defensiveness and see if it is born out of insecurity with your own position and/or from lack of knowledge about the subject.

I have been mystified, confused, angered, astounded, enlightened, and left incredulous by training theories and trainers' explanations. However, especially in the beginning, I would secretly take these feelings as a trigger and study the style or statements for any relevance.

If I discounted a riding theory or system, it was not until I had actually tried to ride or train horses that way. In the beginning, especially being American, I didn't have any particular loyalty to any national system. I was interested in what worked, and if it did work, why.

I began to see that, very often, the power of theories comes more from the charisma, political position, or emotion of the trainer than it does from content. Many riding theories do not make sense. After years of observation of riding lessons at all levels, I have realized that there is little connection between the quality of the advice and the level of the skill of the rider/teacher. Many excellent riders have little capacity to pass on what they *do* to students. In some cases, there almost seems to be an inverse relationship in that, the more naturally gifted the rider is, the less they understand the mechanics of their own process. After studying films and making first-hand observations, I have concluded that, often, the advice of such instructors directly contradicts what they actually do themselves. It is not easy to try to find out what is actually happening, or to point the way to what should be happening.

I have witnessed a series of lessons by a world-class rider/trainer who insisted his student lower his hands. The horse, within a matter of minutes, started falling more and more on the forehand. The trainer asked the student to get down and he got on the horse. He immediately raised his own hands and, with a series of half-halts, he rebalanced the horse. The student remounted and the trainer insisted again that he lower his hands – the horse promptly went back on the forehand. This process continued for several days of my observation, with the level of each participant increasing in frustration.

Alois Podhajsky was the Director of the Spanish Riding School. In his book *The Complete Training of the Horse and Rider*[17] he states: 'There is no need to discuss Guérinière's teachings in detail in this book, not because they are not sufficiently interesting, but because they are applied unaltered at the Spanish Riding School and may be seen there in daily use.'

De la Guérinière himself, in his book *School of Horsemanship*[18], states:

> It is a mistake to let riders do airs above the ground too early, before they have learned to maintain balance at the trot by strengthening the thighs, in order to hold their seat in the saddle. Those who aspire too quickly to jumping take the bad habit of holding their seat with the calves and heels, and upon leaving the riding school they never fail with their supposed skill to be embarrassed when riding young horses. It is by degrees that a rider gains this firmness of seat, which must proceed from equilibrium, and not from the iron grip of calves and heels, which should be left to rough riding jockeys.

[17] A. Podhajsky, *The Complete Training of Horse and Rider*, Wilshire Book Company, 1974.
[18] F.R. de la Guérinière, *School of Horsemanship*, translated by Tracy Boucher, J.A. Allen, 1994.

68

In spite of this clear instruction, there are certain riders from the Spanish Riding School who tell pupils to take their thighs off the horse and hold on with their calves, even though these same riders can ride an air above the ground with no stirrups, only holding on at this movement by the strength of their thighs.

Passionate riders suspend rules of logic and physics. Passionate scientists have little or no experience in training or riding movements, so they discount intuitive 'feel' or athletic differences. We need each other to sort out the material.

People look at da Vinci's drawings of helicopters and think that da Vinci invented the helicopter. Da Vinci never made a helicopter that could fly. It would take several hundred years of seemingly plodding work by scientists and engineers to actually make a helicopter that could fly. Sometimes equestrian writers and equestrian explainers too easily make the jump from what they imagine to what is actually going on.

If you want to build a bridge on the planet earth, you can enlist all types of architectural designs but in the end, they will be based on the fundamental principles of Newtonian physics. If they are not carefully integrated into the design, the bridge may fall down.[19] The longer I train horses, the more I believe there are not infinite methodologies that will produce a sound, collected dressage horse. In fact, because of the evolution of the horse's body – which has been more or less at a steady state throughout the history of riding – and because the relationship between the rider's body and the horse's body presents certain biomechanical requirements or challenges, *very few will work.*

In July of 2003 I had participated in another study at the

[19] Extrapolated from M. Levy and M. Salvadori, *Why Buildings Fall Down,* W.W. Norton & Company, 2002.

McPhail Center. Dr. Clayton designed this study to 'evaluate the effect of collection on ground reaction forces, measured by the force platform. They would indicate just how much weight each limb is carrying and how much propulsion it is providing.'[20] A motion analysis system would track reflective markers that were placed on key areas of the horse to measure the angles of the horse's trunk, neck and head in both the collected trot and a trot purposely ridden on the forehand.

In this study, I did not train the stallion I was riding and I remember clearly that I could not get the quality of collection I would have liked. I remember that the horse was hovering in the collected trot, which stiffened his back and seemed to lock us down on his shoulders. In all fairness, we were new to each other and we might not have been clicking.

To me, the study was very interesting from a visual perspective. The horse did all the things you read about in order to show collection. The motion analysis showed that the horse shortened the overall length of his stride, lowered his haunches as a result of more compression of the hind limbs, visibly increasing the angles of the hind legs. The forehand and neck were more elevated in the collected trot, his poll was the highest point and his nose was about 10 degrees in front of vertical. It was a classical position meeting the requirements of an 'on the bit'[21] posture practically to the letter. To give you some contrast, when I rode him purposely more on the forehand – by not supporting with my back and by lowering my hands, not framing him between the driving and restraining aids – his neck

[20] H. Clayton, 'The mysteries of collection', *USDF Veterinary Connection*, July 2007.
[21] FEI description of 'on the bit', FEI rules.

dropped in elevation, the third vertebra, not the poll, became the highest point and his face was now 10 degrees behind the vertical. Please remember this is documented and measured under the aid of computers.

From my point of view, the more interesting part was the analysis from the force plate which essentially first proved that the horse did carry more weight on the hind legs as he went into the collected trot compared to the trot on the forehand. However, the findings also showed there was not a reciprocal unloading of the forelegs, a simple tipping backwards with a reduction in force on the forelegs and an increase on the hind legs. There was an increase in force on the forelegs as well. In order for this horse to collect, he generated more force both front and back.

If we go back to the definition of bascule – a counterbalanced device that pivots on a central axis so that the unweighted end rises as the weighted end is allowed to fall – that is not what was happening here.

A couple of things come to mind; first is that the outward appearance can fool someone watching. When people ask how competition judges can miss things like whether a given horse is on the forehand, this is how. As Dr. Clayton stated in the study:

> The expected kinematic changes that took place during the collected trot confirmed our *subjective* impressions [my emphasis] of the effects of collection. The ground reaction forces, however, are *not visible* [my emphasis] to the observer. The horse can change the way his hooves push against the ground by altering the muscle tension without causing any change to the kinematics. The vertical and longitudinal

forces indicate the horse's degree of balance and the functional responsibilities of his front and hind limbs.

So it is not always obvious to the viewer what the horse is actually doing.

The second thing that comes to mind is that this is not the description of the piaffe to levade study, which showed no increase in force off the forelimbs to lift the forehand and supremely collect the horse. I can tell you that one of the reasons why I wanted to bring my horse St. Graal and measure those forces again was because I was bothered by results of the first study. Although the kinematics of the horse in the first study were correct I, as the rider, felt that the balance was wrong. As a rider this is one of the things you must learn to feel: the true balance of the horse.

I think Dr. Clayton has already alluded to one explanation of the apparent discrepancies of these two studies when she talked about how the balance of the horse is different with different individual horses.[22] If a lot of studies were done, I am certain they would show that some horses, like some people, have naturally better balance than others, and they will be more athletic, more intelligent as Howard Garner[23] might say, in the bodily kinesthetic domain. I would add that starting off with ordinary balance does not preclude a horse from improving it.

There are also some important differences in the two studies, for example, if you are already in piaffe and further collect to the levade the horse is not moving forward very much, so the braking forces on the fore- and hind limbs will naturally

[22] H. Clayton, 'What is biomechanics', *The Hanoverian Magazine*, Fall 1999.
[23] H. Garner, *The Unschooled Mind*, Basic Books, 1991.

be much smaller than if you are collecting the trot from a working trot or extended trot.

I think that, as in the terre-à-terre at the canter, in the trot the horse will also bound off the forehand at times to help in elevating and setting up the collection and coiling; the forelimbs supporting the horse while the hind legs come under. Good riders are aware of this and try for a balance shift more oriented to the muscles of the back, abdomen and hindquarters. These riders actually make their seats light and their backs strong, and the contact will be passive and limiting in order to block the horse from falling further forward and to allow the hindquarters to come under. There is always talk about lightness of hands, lightness in the hands. I have explained many times that, depending on the horse, the contact will sometimes be relatively heavy if the horse tries to fall forward and the rider blocks this with the reins and their back and seat. Many teachers abhor any weight in the reins. Some solve the problem by using special and severe bits, or sensitizing the horse's mouth so that it will yield from pressure at what are extremely sensitive pressure points, very martial arts-like. Yielding like this has nothing to do with lightening the forehand by putting the horse upon the haunches. I myself hate heavy contact. However, in order to correct it, one has to realize that there is a very big difference between pulling on the reins (i.e. rider aggression), and fixing the length of rein to stop the horse from pulling (i.e. horse aggression). In the dressage that I subscribe to, no one gets to pull. Setting legitimate boundaries works in two ways. One is physical: blocking the tendency of the horse to balance naturally on the forehand and introducing a new technique that takes advantage of the huge muscles behind to balance more on the back end. The second is psychological: it reinforces the rider's authority as leader. Without this kind of riding, the ambivalence the rider is telegraphing is, in the horse's eyes, equal to weakness or, at the very least, an opening for negotiation – mostly at inopportune times.

The backs of good riders are strong and they are connected to their legs for the maximum leverage, but their seats might be light to allow the horse to flex at the lumbo-sacral joint, and not push it down in any way to lock out the hindquarters. I think it was Egon von Neindorff who said, 'Sometimes the rider has to feel like they could slip a sheet of paper under their seat bones.' When the hind legs are sufficiently under and in place to carry, the rider tries to maintain the balance with techniques like half-halts, etc., in order to continue to develop this tipping back.[24]

At the McPhail Center, I was also part of one study in which I was fitted with rein tension sensors, electronically recording pressure in each rein. As I was riding, I could actually see the large graph on the side of the arena. If the horse or rider pulled, the graph line would spike, leaving a record on the graph, like mini seismic recordings. As I remember there were two jagged lines: two graphs of different colours, one for my right hand and another for my left. If you had looked at the graph after I finished, you would have seen the recording starting by spiking pretty hard and gradually getting lighter. In fact, the spikes peaked around 5 lb (2.25 kg), and decreased to about 1 lb (0.45 kg). By looking at the graph you might assume that I was taking repetitive half-halts, or making corrections, but that was not the case. I noticed while riding that the spikes were occurring in time with the stance phase of the trot, or when the foreleg (and of

[24] For more information please see: P. Belasik, *Dressage for the 21st Century*, J.A. Allen, 2001.

.

course its diagonally partnered hind leg) hit the ground. I knew what I was doing. The horse started out heavy on the forehand; each time he landed he tried to fall forward. I blocked this with a passive hand and supported my hand with my back, seat and thighs. My hand was still. The spike was occurring from the horse hitting the bit and reins. I really did nothing but set the boundary and held my position as steady and strong and quiet as I could, and as we went on the horse began to figure it out and to avoid hitting the bit, began to balance more toward the rear. I was not pulling on the reins, but by me setting limits the horse corrected himself. The graph needed analysis. Another case of what you see might not be what is actually happening.

A second significant result was that some riders thought 3 lb (1.36 kg) of weight in the hands was horrible; it should be light as a feather; reins of silk. This, by the way, was a Warmblood stallion who weighed about 1,500 lb (680 kg), whom I had never ridden before. Afterwards, I went to a fishing tackle store and bought some 5 lb and 10 lb (2.25 and 4.5 kg) test fishing line and, as I remember, I had a hard time even finding 1 lb (0.45 kg) test line. In some subsequent lectures, I made loops of three different weights of line and attached them to a pair of reins. Then I let riders break them. I am not sure anyone present would have wanted to try to ride all the high-school exercises on a game horse with a link of 2lb (0.9 kg) test fishing line between the bit and the reins. Many riders have no real idea what kind of forces we are talking about, and too many authors have been too free with poetic licence. If you tie a 4 lb (1.8 kg) test link of line between the reins and an average full bridle, and you drop the bridle itself with no horse in it and try to stop it before it hits the floor by holding the reins, the line will break from the weight of the bridle alone: 4 lb (1.8 kg) is quite light.

We sometimes need to take advantage of the science of the day to get realistic appraisals of what we are trying to do. Impossible suggestions from educators will only frustrate equine and human pupils.

There will be many times – in fact, most of the time in riding – when the balance will not be correct. The classical rider's mantra will be to stay committed and learn the exercises, be consistent and use them to improve this. Classical riding is all about the process, not goals. Along the way you are learning emotional control, patience with insight, and physical fitness. Sometimes, the pragmatic goals of training a horse to a certain level are beyond your controls (the horse gets injured in the pasture). However, the effort you apply to your practice is not. With constant, correct practice, the balance will improve and learning how to change the range of balance from long and low, to piaffe and to a levade will become easier.

Naïve riders are unaware of this balance shift – usually because their position is so poor they can't feel it – or they might feel it but can't do anything constructive about it, so they let the horse fall through the reins. Sophisticated poor riders learn to fake it and develop theories and styles of riding that have no impulsion; their motto seems to be: 'We're going nowhere, but we're going lightly.' Other poor riders drive their horses backs down with a heavy seat; the hind end gets locked out behind and can't come under for leverage, no matter how fast these riders chase the hind legs, or ride their horses forward. Probably the worse of all riders are ones who know better but who gloss over bad technique because of a competition schedule or performance agenda, or to patronize students.

I have said many times that dressage is good for all horses, but I have never said that all horses are good for dressage. I feel that almost all horses' balance can be improved through use of the proper exercises, but some horses will be severely limited by their conformation, attitude, etc., as to how far they can go toward achieving the best kind of balanced collection. A good attitude to work can, however, overcome immense impediments.

One of my horses – St. Graal in fact – was born croup-high with a long back; he had probably the poorest conformation of any of my own horses. There were many times when I felt that his conformation would limit him, but he had an enormous heart. He would never quit. For my part, I had faith that the classical exercises would work if I executed them correctly and if I didn't ignore bad technique – his or mine. He turned out to be a real artist. These experiences have been borne out again and again in the training of countless horses with conformational and emotional and mental limitations, both by me and others.

CHAPTER 8

The Exercises

Although the levade is one proof that a horse and rider have mastered the art of collecting – that they have learned to elevate the forehand without an excessive bounding off the forelegs – you obviously cannot *start* training at the levade. A series of exercises have developed to teach collection. These exercises can have multiple benefits, for example, suppling a horse left and right, but I want to address here their principle benefit – collection – and how they need to be ridden to develop that collection.

The Shoulder-in

A student of mine came back excited after participating in a clinic with one of the younger riders in a world-famous riding school. She was beaming in particular, as she said, 'I rode the biggest shoulder-in that I have ever ridden in my life. I had no idea I could ride that big. He said: "More and more", and I did it. My horse was amazing, people watching were so impressed.' The trainer should have known better. In *The*

Dynamic Horse, Dr. Hilary Clayton makes the following observation:

> Some horses naturally place the hind limb further forward beneath the trunk but contrary to the opinion of many trainers, hind limb protraction does not increase with collection. Horses do not step further underneath themselves in the collected gaits. What actually changes is the hind limbs do not push out so far behind the horse.

The more you ask for protraction, the more the hind limb stays out behind; it is a simple pendulum. Essentially, the longer the step, the further you go away from collection.

The shoulder-in is a pre-eminent lateral exercise; its creation is credited to the French trainer de la Guérinière. His work was based partially on work by the Duke of Newcastle, to whom he gives credit: if you read both men's work you will see the evolution of the exercises. One key point about the exercise is that bigger is not necessarily better.

De la Guérinière had a pretty sophisticated view of collection, which can be seen when he talks about the use of the pillars and how hock engagement alone will not make a horse balance (collect) onto the haunches:

> The Duke of Newcastle is not in favour of the pillars. Newcastle says: 'One tires and torments a horse in the pillars to no purpose, making it lift the forehand and hoping thereby to put it on its haunches. This method is against the natural order and mortifies all horses. The pillars put the horse on its hocks, for although it bends the hocks, it does

not advance the haunches to keep equilibrium, but supports the forehand with the ropes of the cavesson!' [De la Guérinière continues] This illustrious author revolted against the pillars because in this time most horsemen used them to teach the horse to raise the forehand without proper training in the piaffe. In so doing they doubtless put the horse on its hocks and taught it to prance and to go on tip toes rather than raise the forehand with grace.[25]

It is clear he is talking about learning to lift the forehand without leaning on anything, but with a balanced grace and strength. De la Guérinière knew that hock action is not synonymous with collection. Collection is synonymous with the ability to lift easily, or, as we often say today, carry. This carrying involves the back, abdomen, psoas, etc. I think many people use the terms 'collection', 'engagement' and 'flexion' interchangeably, and this is confusing. Some writer/trainers will refer to engagement as being the protraction of the hind leg. More engagement here means more reach under the body. We know now from current biomechanics that collection occurs when there is a shorter protraction and retraction; a shorter stroke of the hind legs. I think in this case it is probably wise to yield to the scientific language, and if you want more or less reach, use 'reach' or 'protraction,' instead of 'engagement,' or else be clear to define your terms.

Other writer/trainers use 'engagement' to describe flexion of the hocks, stifles, hips and the hind limbs; think of a horse picking his hind legs up over cavalletti. However, as de la

[25] F.R. de la Guérinière, *School of Horsemanship*, translated by Tracy Boucher, J.A. Allen, 1994.

Guérinière so carefully described, you cannot assume that increased flexion or engagement is synonymous with collection. Many pressed horses will show more and more flexion in the hind limb joints, but if this increased activity is a result of leaning on the reins attached to the pillars or the rider's hands, or if it becomes so active that the horse supports it by balancing on his forelegs, it becomes the opposite of collection, which is the ability to lift the forehand. A sleepy horse may be asked for more engagement, which could lead to better collection, but if the engagement becomes excessive it will move away from collection to a balance on the forehand. So engagement is not synonymous with collection.

The shoulder-in was one of the first and foremost exercises employed to teach this collection. De la Guérinière wrote of it: 'This exercise has so many benefits I regard it as the alpha and omega of all exercises for the horse.'[26] In the shoulder-in, which is usually ridden along the wall of the school, the horse moves on a bias along the wall. The rider initiates the curve 'with inside rein and leg',[27] and then uses the push of the inside leg to signal the horse to move slightly sideways. When the shoulders are off the wall, the torso of the horse is directly in front of the path of the inside hind leg so when this leg steps forward, it steps under the mass. This leg will take an inordinate load as it lifts the mass and pushes it on a bias parallel to the wall. The outside rein is used to prevent the horse from bending the neck too much or putting too much curve in the body. If the exercise were ridden

[26] F.R. de la Guérinière, *School of Horsemanship*, translated by Tracy Boucher, J.A. Allen, 1994.
[27] F.R. de la Guérinière, *School of Horsemanship*, translated by Tracy Boucher, J.A. Allen, 1994.

in the open, the rider's outside leg would take the place of the wall, and prevent the hindquarters from stepping out, losing the curve and straightening the body as in leg-yielding.

The shoulder-in is such a wonderful exercise because you can isolate the stiffer or less dexterous side of the horse and build up the coordination, while you are teaching the horse to lower that hip and step under the weight. If you ride the shoulder-in bigger and bigger, you risk having the inside hind leg step past the centre of mass, making it difficult, if not impossible, to lift. The hind leg, because it gets left further out behind each stride, also facilitates the dropping of the back (think of the 'park horse' stance where the feet get stretched out too far to the front and too far to the rear, or of when a male horse urinates). The more sag in the back and letting go in the abdominals, the less the ability to bascule. The hind legs only seem to run, chasing the inertia with exaggerated hock action, trying to catch up.

So, when de la Guérinière created the shoulder-in exercise, he had quite specific requirements. These requirements turn out to be quite accurately supported in terms of the most current biomechanical research. So why do people insist on adjusting it? I think exercises tend to evolve. One reason for this is that new information becomes available. Scientists invent new machines to collect more data. Somewhere along the way, a camera is invented which evolves toward high-speed filming, which uncovers new evidence of how something works. The new evidence gets incorporated in previous work to yield a better result.

When I was on sport teams when I was younger, we often did callisthenics as a warm-up and to aid strength training. We often did sit-ups to improve abdominal strength. One person would hold the knees of the other down against the hard floor while the person on the floor did repetitive sit-ups. It turns out that doing sit-ups this way puts a lot of strain on the lower back and instead of helping, they can do harm. It was argued that if you bent your knees and did crunches/abdominal contractions, you would get all the value out of working the abdominals without the risk to the lower back. This is now the normal way these exercises are executed. Through a scientific approach the technique improves and the benefits of the exercise or activity are maximized.

However, there is another reason why exercises evolve, and that is through imitation and embellishment. One sees an activity and it gets copied: as time goes on, a little flair is added here or there. Often, there is really very little serious argument or evidence or thinking in this evolution. The element of improvement is highly subjective.

A person I know was on a football team quite a few years ago. Someone on the team found out about some pills which could quickly and substantially add muscle mass and strength. The coaches approved and within a short time virtually everyone on the team was taking what we know now to be steroids. No one seriously researched possible side-effects; the results were too seductive.

Certain techniques in martial arts and dance start with the imitation of a particular form. In a comparative and competitive way, the participant tries to stand out with a slightly higher kick, a little more speed, a little more extension. Participants ignore serious pain to reap the rewards of the embellishment, until there is a host of relatively young people requiring hip and knee surgery.

In saddle-seat riding of gaited horses, what started as a way of riding smoothly across country has evolved into a discipline in which virtually every aspect has gone too far. The tails are so long that the horses can never use them because they are always protected in a bag. The feet are too long because the unnatural and weighted shoes embellish the action of the horses' limbs. The heads are too high, dropping the backs too low. The saddles sit too far back. The rider's stirrup leathers are too long. Everything becomes artifice and a parody of its original design. Discomfort, lameness, and other side-effects are ignored. A tangent develops away from the core and gains strength; convinced by its own hubris, it ignores any beneficial input that might correct it.

Riders have to be careful to monitor their technique so that it is sound in its fundamentals. Trainers need to consciously analyse the horse's technique for signs of artifice, and keep constantly in mind the objectives of the exercise. Remember, if you live in a foreign country for a while it is easy to develop that accent unconsciously. It is easy to follow the people around you; like the horses, we want to fit in. It is a strong force and not always healthy for the individual.

When riders practise the shoulder-in there are some consistent mistakes which have a direct effect on the ability to indicate collection. One is that, for most people and horses, you are matching up the less dexterous side of the horse with the less dexterous side of the human, namely the left (obviously, it can be the opposite). When the horse and rider begin the left shoulder-in, riders commonly drop their left hand down and pull on the rein. The combined braking effect of the rein and the downward angle encourages the horse's mass to fall directly onto the left shoulder, which is the very part we are trying to lighten and raise up. The second most common mistake is that the rider will use the outside rein to displace the shoulders to the inside as in neck-reining. Again, the rein effects brake the impulsion and tip the balance further onto the forelegs, in this case with the added risk of taking the bend out of the body and turning the exercise into leg-yielding. The rider has to practise coordinating the use of their own inside leg to get the horse to use his inside hind leg. As soon as the rider presses the leg against the barrel of the horse there has to be a concession. The inside rein helps set up the bend but it should not go down (unless the horse was way above the bit), but stay at the same level or be raised slightly, both to remind the horse to stay flexed at the poll and to feel if the weight is shifting the wrong way. The weight of the rider has to lead the movement. It is easy to fall behind it if the horse is a little reluctant and the rider uses more leg pressure. If the rider tries to too hard they end up contracting the whole inside of their body, changing their weight distribution and almost dragging the horse backwards.

The shoulder-in is the embodiment of the axiom 'inside leg to outside rein', always in that order. When it is correct it feels as if the horse is going up a wide circular staircase. The forehand and shoulders are up ahead higher, being lifted, as if were, by the inside hind leg.

The shoulder-in is so useful for beginning to teach collection because, by isolating just one leg at a time, it isn't so physically demanding that the horse will get upset.

After you have met the initial requirements of correct bend (i.e. tracking neither too much nor too little) and correct profile (i.e. not above the bit, not behind the bit), the most important point in the execution will be the size and the direction of the steps. If you push the hind leg too much it may step past the centre of mass and make it impossible to collect. If you don't push the hind leg enough, it won't get under the mass and won't be able to develop any lift or strength and, even with years of practice, you won't be any closer to collection.

Entrances and Exits:
A Quest for Elegant Exercises

Many times, the choreography of entering and exiting and placing a particular exercise can override the *value* of the exercise. Successful choreography is driven by biomechanics and physics. For example, there is really is no such thing as a counter shoulder-in. If you were going straight down the centre line, away from any wall, or were out in a large field and developed a shoulder-in, you would develop either a shoulder-in to the left or a shoulder-in to the right. That is all de la Guérinière created. Some trainers will go down the long wall in a left direction, that is, entering it through the corner counter-clockwise, and then develop a right shoulder-in after they have come through the first left turn. In order to do this, you have to use your right leg to swing the haunches toward the middle of the arena but, unlike the travers where you have some bend with the preceding corner, you have to change the bend. If you try it, you will see it is an awkward set-up that almost invariably disengages the hindquarters when they fishtail to the inside. The resulting shoulder-in is a right shoulder-in along the wall. Compare this to the logical set-up of a normal shoulder-in (where, after coming through the corner bent to the left, you then use a little more inside leg and intensify the position and then hold it steady on a bend with the outside aids.) When you make this comparison, the idea of changing the shoulder-in or doing a so-called right shoulder-in going to the left seems purposefully disingenuous, tricky, and unduly complicated.

The best choreography always strives for an elegance 'often ingeniously neat, simple, or concise.'[28] In certain cases, however, the choreography is complicated because of simple considerations of physics. For example, many trainers try to use the shoulder-in on a circle. Here, the rider is applying the inside leg while turning. It takes an extremely good rider to execute this effectively because of the simple problem of centrifugal force. As the horse is turning, a force is produced pushing to the outside of the circle. The rider plays into these forces and 'begs' the horse to drift by adding their own aids to increase the natural outside drift. To combat this, the rider has to use a lot of outside rein and outside leg to prevent the slide, until the exercise is really more like renvers. The outside hind leg does the most work – which is completely the opposite of the initial intention to work the inside hind leg with the shoulder-in. Mistakes in choices of choreography can lead to opposite effects. Legitimate exercises can be constructive or destructive simply in their placement during practice.

Travers and Renvers

The travers and renvers, as I have said elsewhere, are clone exercises. They really are the same exercise except in their

[28] A.H. Soukhanov (US General Editor), et al., *Encarta World English Dictionary*, St. Martin's Press, 1999.

reference to a wall. In the travers, the haunches are away from the wall; the shoulders are on the wall. In the renvers, the haunches are on the wall and the shoulders are off. Both have logical entrances and exits.

Let's say we are tracking to the left around the riding school. As we enter a corner the horse is bent to the left; as the shoulders of the horse are about to move down the long wall, we keep the bend started in the corner. We leave the shoulders parallel to the wall and, with our outside leg, ask the hindquarters to move toward the middle of the arena. In terms of collection, the size of the step and the tracking are important. If the hindquarters are in too far, the 'motor' in a sense fishtails as in a car: the power slips away; there is no propulsion, the energy escapes in a spin. If the hindquarters are in too far, the outside hind leg can't step under the mass of the horse to aid in weight-carrying; instead it steps beyond the centre of mass. Ideally, as in the shoulder-in, the hind legs want to step in approximately three tracks so the outside hind leg, which is driving the travers, will also carry the travers. However, even if the alignment is fairly correct but the rider asks for too long a step, the hind leg will stay out behind the horse too long and compromise its ability to carry more weight. Furthermore, the step can reach past the centre of mass and frustrate attempts to lift with the back, abdomen and rear. So the amount of bend is very important to facilitate the muscular action which will eventually be able to lift the front end.

For an example of elegant choreography, compare the travers on a circle to the shoulder-in on the circle. In the travers, the rider is using the outside leg to get the horse to step in with their outside hind leg. The outside rein supports, but should not pull the movement in. Now the natural centrifugal force is logically addressed by the outside aids, with the bonus of using this extra resistance (as opposed to doing the travers on a straight line where there is no centrifugal force) as part of an increasingly difficult training strategy. This kind of exercise is a perfect introduction to the aids and feeling of the pirouette. It addresses logically the pitfalls of centrifugal force, and uses it for benefit.

The renvers presents the trainer with more complex choices. Here, the trainer can use a counter-bend to help gymnasticize the horse, by juxtaposing true and counter-bend fairly quickly to block persistent resistances or evasions by the horse. Remember, these are not neck bends. The beauty of the renvers is that you can get the benefit of changing bend without swinging the haunches all over. For example, once again we're tracking left around the arena. We turn left through a corner and enter a shoulder-in left. The left hind leg steps under the mass; we are aware of its collecting ability. Halfway down the long wall we switch to renvers; the haunches stay along the wall, the shoulders stay off, but now we change from left bend to right bend. The horse's body must be free of resistance yet the left hind leg still drives the movement. The complexity challenges the horse's suppleness without risking losing control of the hindquarters.

Now, it is *possible* to change bend from travers to renvers. If you again are on the left rein in haunches-in or travers, the right hind leg drives and carries the movement. Halfway down the long wall you switch the bend to the right and change to renvers, but now the horse must swing his haunches into the arena and change the drive leg to the left hind. However, every time you swing the haunches like that you risk losing the connection through the middle of the horse. As discussed earlier, no matter how good the front end is or how good the back end is, if you can't connect the two, bascule and collection will be impossible. Furthermore, when you change drive legs like that mid-wall, there is always a moment of almost tripping as the horse kind of skips onto the other leg.

Whenever you can attack problems with simple solutions, you maximize the effectiveness of training and minimize the chance of actually introducing your horse to bad habits by accident. If you confuse neck-bending with the gymnastic effects of truly bending and counter-bending the body in logical choreography, you can inadvertently do just that. Later, when you try for the highest degrees of collection, the horse will need to be straight and connected in order to truly bascule and lift for the airs. If you have shown the horse ways to cock the neck from one side to other, to avoid rein pressure, you will have created your own monster. Later, you may find that the horse evades collection by slight twists in the neck and lets energy out of one shoulder or the other, and you can never seem to make him 'of one piece'.

Half-pass

If you have had the good fortune to study under a classical dressage master, or if you are a student of that literature, you will have come across the term 'circus'. It is never a compliment. This is not really a personal indictment. I know that there were many classical dressage trainers who were friends of great circus trainers, and they respected each other's work. They knew though, that their work was different. In the circus, the reason for being is entertainment; the rapport with the audience is crucial, the reaction of the audience is paramount. The goal is to thrill, amaze, to induce rapture or wonder. To be a successful circus trainer you must be admired by the public, or you will be out of a job. For some circus performers their work is motivated by wonder and joy; at its worst, it is motivated by narcissism and undeveloped personalities.

In the art of classical riding, the audience's reaction is not the reason for being. The audience is, in a sense, invited to observe a performance, which in the performance arts would be a demonstration of the creative process. The artist creates something, but not necessarily for us, the observers. There have been many successful and important artists who were unknown to the general public; it isn't necessary to be admired by the public to a successful artist.

The art or artistic performance has some serious underpinnings in years of practice and study of technique. An artist might display virtuosity, but even if this virtuosity is spectacular, if it is flawed by poor technique the work could be deemed incomplete, unfinished, by other artists, aficionados, or teachers. This leads us to the question: is this what directs artists – the judgement of their peers? Instead of the paying public audience, some external review board? Is this why artists practise and practise, often alone? I think the answer is the opposite. The limits of an artistic expression or performance are not just the limits of an artist's imagination. The limits are often technique. As when an artist has an idea of doing something in their mind but they haven't enough skill, discipline or courage to execute it or express it, to make it come alive.

Artists know this. This is why, when they are in mentoring

capacities, they care about technique in other artists. They want them to succeed. They do not want them to be frustrated, unable to go where they want to because of lack of technique. In some ways it can be selfish; they want to be inspired by other artists so their own work can advance. It is not about externally applied, arbitrary subjective requirements. It is more about correcting techniques that will otherwise eventually limit self-expression.

The moments when artistic expressions are made to come alive can be inspirational. An audience may get to watch, but they aren't really participating (not that they can't have effects with their negative or positive response). For various reasons, many pieces of writing, or paintings, come to the public's attention years after they were complete. By then, the artist is doing something completely different.

When classical dressage masters made the distinction between circus and classical dressage this is what they were referring to. It is easy to amaze the audience; it is going to be much harder to amaze yourself. Embark on the process, study technique to express yourself better; you will best serve society in the fullest completion of yourself. Observe art not vicariously but as inspiration for your own work. Become an artist.

What has this got to do with the half-pass? Everything. Today, among a lot of dressage practitioners, the line between circus and classical dressage is getting purposefully blurred. All riders love to say that they train by the classical principles, yet it is clear that many are not working on their technique. Many get failing grades in terms of understanding the biomechanics or the choreography of the dressage exercises. Many are really just interested in winning prizes and competing – which is fine, but like the older circus riders and classical dressage riders, you have to know the difference. This psychological ambivalence serves neither form of riding. I can't tell you how many riders I meet who say: 'I want to ride on the Olympic team.' They don't say they want to learn to ride well. Who is teaching them this? What do *you* really want – to ride very well or to improve your status, to be a celebrity?

When you ride the half-pass and you ride it to make it stand out – faster and bigger – the horse has a tendency to create more push off from the forelegs. This greater ground reaction force bounces the forelegs up. It can look very flashy, but it necessitates putting more weight onto the forehand – the opposite of true collection, which always has the concept of bascule as an objective. The half-pass should not be ridden with such long steps that the horse can't gather himself. The hind leg that drives the half-pass should try to step under the mass in order to lift. The horse's body should not be bent so much that the connecting mid-section – the abdominals, back, etc. – are compromised by being stretched too far. It should not be ridden so fast that the hind leg steps past the centre of mass and stays out behind the horse for too much of the stride, unable to carry weight.

Longitudinal Exercises

The longitudinal exercises refer to exercises where the horse is 'straight', even though they can be executed on curved lines: essentially, we distinguish them from the lateral exercises. In the walk, the range is from collected walk to extended walk. In the trot, it is from the form represented by piaffe to extended trot. In the canter, from pirouette or school canter to extended canter. (I have discussed the gaits and their variants in detail in other books.)

It would be easy to assume that, in order to develop collection which would lead to the airs, one would practise a lot in the collected gaits. To a certain extent, this is true – provided that the rider understands what 'collected' feels like. However, it's often through the shrewd juxtaposition of a variety of exercises that the horse is gymnasticized and builds the best kind of strength.

Since collection is strenuous, it is understandable why horses might avoid it or adjust it, or 'cheat' on the exercise. Riders have to be able to feel this and limit it. Unfortunately today, some riders are encouraging it.

The challenge of collection – especially in any transitions into it – is that the forelimbs of the horse come into play. We know that there are considerable 'negative or braking forces'[29] on the forelimbs when the horse collects. To me, these are inevitable because the horse is a quadruped. Take the canter for example: there is a moment in the stride where, as the horse collects, both hind legs will be off the ground and surging forward under the mass. It's obvious that, if the forelimbs (or limb) did not support the horse while he was bringing his hind legs under, the horse would fall down. Even in the trot there is this support phase during which, over a series of repetitive strides, the hind legs can ratchet a little further under and position themselves to lift. Think of a weightlifter rocking back and forth to get their stance just right before they lift. With their arms, yes, but mainly they lift with their backs, abdominals and legs.

[29] H. Clayton, 'The mysteries of collection', *USDF Connection*, July 2003.

In collection, we know it's possible for the horse to elevate the shoulders and withers by increasing the ground reaction forces on the forelimbs. Horses can actually push off with their forelimbs, showing an 'uphill' profile, but not necessarily doing it by lifting the forelegs as in the levade, but rather incorrectly, as in balancé.

To me, this becomes the quintessential dilemma while riding to try to develop the muscle system for a collection that will logically lead to a levade. You have to try to limit the horse from helping too much with the front end when you are trying for more collection.

In an effort to add flair to the front end work of the horse, many riders today are inadvertently trying to exaggerate the support phase of the forelegs and turn it into a more and more active impulsion phase. When they do this, the hind end will be lower and it may even carry more weight because the horse is collecting from the previous trot. The problem is that the overall ratio of weight distribution is not tipping toward the rear; it is going even further to the front, as the horse pushes off the ground more and more with the forelimbs to show more and more exaggerated foreleg work. It is very reminiscent of the hunter riders who learned to 'bury' the horse on the forehand before the fence and then marvelled how even an average mover would yank his forelegs up to avoid hitting the fence, showing this same exaggerated style. Riding a dressage horse deeper on the front end, adding more weight to get a bigger ground reaction force, can have this same effect.

If you watch the better riders of the Spanish Riding School at a performance in the collected trot and you compare some of the current winning competitors at their collected trot, you will see two very different trots. At first, one can say the biggest difference is the size of the gait. To me, however, it is much more than that; the balance is the difference. From the shorter collected trot at the Spanish Riding School, the horses develop to produce the best airs in the world. These riders are taught to aim their training in that direction. The mock rears of exuberant young horses are not always bad evasions; sometimes they are uneducated experiments with balance – but the balance is to the rear. This will be encouraged, controlled and developed, whereas many other riders have become obsessed with size of gait which has led to the 'forehand' trots we are seeing today.

The rider/trainer first has to realize that this is the effect if you purposefully exaggerate the forehand push-off – it amounts to a kind of circus balancé and that practice is the antithesis of classical collection. If this is happening and you want to correct it you have to try to get the horse to feel as if he will rear. I am not encouraging anyone to teach resistant, ill-behaved rearing. I am saying that the art is to learn to control that feeling. So, as you ride the collected trot, try to learn to feel those slight shifts to the rear and encourage them. Above all, don't keep pushing the horse further onto the forelimbs, where he will never learn to gather the forces of impulsion and pull them up, but will 'bounce' them up.

One of the first times to begin to feel this shift is if you can do trot-halts. The hind legs must be under as the horse gets lighter on the forehand. The neck position is up still and on the bit. If you halt and feel the horse pull down with his neck you are not getting it. If you halt with energy and the hocks are buried in the tail, you are not getting it. If you halt and then the horse steps up, no again. If you halt and he backs up out of the shape, no. If you persist in using your back and seat to block the pulling, and if you ride in with good power, you will begin to understand the feeling of the horse answering your seat and leg. If the horse gets too light in front and mock rears, make sure this is not lack of submission to the bridle, but just a lack of 'throughness'. If it is a lack of submission, you may need to do in-hand work to challenge the horse safely. However, if the horse tips up a little too far, but is soft in the hand, you are probably on the right track but just a little too aggressive. You must be able to learn this feeling and your horse has to learn to rebalance like this if you want to learn collection.

Piaffe

If one of the first places you begin to feel the shift of weight is in the trot-halt transitions, then one of the last places you train and feel it is in the piaffe. To me, the most important feature of the piaffe is not rhythm; it is weight shift or carrying power. In a sense, the current biomechanical analysis adds to this historical perspective. If we look at the footfalls of the piaffe, we see that there is no moment of suspension. At all times there is at least one foot on the ground. If you are defining the family of trot exercises – collected trot, working trot, medium trot, etc. – the piaffe will not fit into the continuation of trot because all the other trots have a moment of suspension, even if there's slight dissociation, positive or negative. From the standpoint of footfalls or limb patterns, the piaffe is an anomaly. The piaffe clearly exists under a different rhythm of stride. Not only is it different in terms of rhythm within a single stride (there is no moment of suspension) but, also, different horses will show either positive dissociation (the hind foot hits down just before its diagonal partner), or negative dissociation (the forefoot hits down first before its hind limb diagonal partner). Yet they can be pretty good piaffes. Although the classical piaffe should be one with as pure a diagonal relationship as possible, it is clear under close analysis of films that there is great variation.

This does not mean that the piaffe is some arbitrary exercise with no defining objective. The reason is because, as I have said, rhythm is not the definitive feature; weight shift is. If you are defining the family of trot exercises as a continuum of more or less collection, then the piaffe fits perfectly. Whether a particular horse has slight changes in limb patterns is less important than whether the horse 'sits' and balances more on his hind end. This *has* to be the definitive feature, because the piaffe is a preparation for any air above the ground.

The piaffe stores energy and sets up the shift of balance onto the hind legs. The dissociation of the gait is somewhat natural because, for example, as the horse elevates ('rises' as the Duke of Newcastle might have said) from the piaffe and onto his hind legs, he will bring up one foreleg at a time and then match them as in perfect levade or courbette. When the horse comes down from the air back onto the forelegs, they will separate again, landing one at a time.

I am not saying that, in practising the piaffe, you can ignore rhythm. The best piaffes will have both as clear a rhythm as possible and the balance shift, but lightening of the forehand is the primary objective. Likewise, when you are practising the various trots there shouldn't be huge changes in tempo from trot to trot, but primary attention has to be on the range of collection and not on an obsession on the exact placement of the footfalls. We have already seen that description of gaits is often arbitrary.[30] Furthermore, as Doug Leach says:

> There is such a continuum of changes on the limb coordination patterns seen in horses that, when you carefully analyse the locomotion of these animals, clearly there is a whole continuum of changes which these animals are capable of. It is us in our simplified way of analysing these animals that categorize and selectively train for specific gaits. Hildebrand in California has defined over 400 different strides, and from his work he has concluded there is no such thing as stride.[31]

Canter

I was teaching a lesson on one of my school horses to an experienced horsewoman and rider; she was very well educated in sciences. It was our first lesson together: as the lesson progressed, I decided to work on walk to canter, canter to walk transitions. She asked: 'When do you ask for the strike-off?', meaning when what foot was in what position. It almost seems as though there are two fields of attention here. One is a mechanistic thinking, dividing the gaits by footfall patterns, logically assuming that, like gears, the horse will change these patterns with instruction. The second field of attention seems less cognitive (which it isn't) but has to do with feeling. The

[30] P. Belasik, *Exploring Dressage Technique*, J.A. Allen, 1994.
[31] Interview with Doug Leach by author.

transition is set up when the horse feels right. A wild horse might be trotting at a particular speed and then want to move faster; at a certain speed the brain instructs the horse to change to the canter in order do so. When you train a young horse to canter for the first time, you usually use this kind of technique. You press the young horse, even allowing him to fall a little on the forehand and increase speed to 'roll' into the canter. Almost as soon as you do this, as soon as the horse learns this, you begin to adjust the canter and the transition, otherwise you'll encourage the horse to rush through the transition on the forehand instead of balancing a little to the rear. You then try to time your asking for the transition when the horse feels balanced and in control, not leaning into the bridle. This is far more important than which limb is where.

An interesting thing happens over time in training. In something like two-time flying changes, both these fields of attention merge. The rider has to know exactly where the horse's feet are in terms of the particular stride because successful changes will depend on split-second timing. The flying change can only occur at one particular place in the stride pattern. The rider also has to have good 'feel' because even if you hit the exact place, a flying change may still not work correctly. This is especially so in a series, where your horse has to begin in balance and stay in balance until the line of changes, whatever the number, is complete.

The walk to canter and canter to walk transitions are among the first places in the canter where you begin to work on collection. When I taught the lesson just mentioned, I was interested to assess how good this rider's 'feel' was. Since I knew the horse very well, I could learn a lot quickly about placing the rider in terms of skill and experience, and also plan where to go, what to work on in subsequent lessons.

You have to really try to make sure that the horse doesn't lean forward and use his neck by throwing it up or down to help with the balance. The rider tries to keep the front end quiet and get the horse to use his abdominals and hindquarters to step under and carry the transition. It is only natural for the horse to try to use the forehand for the lion's share of balancing. The problem with riding is that it is very unnatural for the horse. The horse has to be taught that what is natural is not necessarily helpful when doing these things carrying the weight of a rider. For me, dressage has always been the only ethical way to train horses for riding. Collection aims at building the bridge from back to front to enhance bascule. The result of this discipline is that the posture/positioning of the back and neck in training for collection make the bridge strong enough to carry the rider with less harm to the structure. The canter pirouette showcases strength and balance; the horse and rider in collection.[32] In a sense it also showcases the problem of integrating science into dressage. There were many heated discussions about whether the pirouette was a three-beat movement similar to a regular canter or whether it was four-beat. Furthermore, whichever it was, what should the rider try for?

By this time, after seeing many films in slow motion of many horses executing pirouettes, I think everyone agrees that it is a four-beat movement. Yet we still have an ideal in mind that dressage movements should not break up the natural rhythms of gait. The walk should try to stay four-beat, the trot

[32] For more information, please see P. Belasik, *Dressage for the 21st Century*, J.A. Allen, 2001.

two-beat and the canter three-beat. In the reality of scientific analysis, we see that even this not necessarily true. The closer you look, the less gaits seem so pure.

I think that the classical advice here was never meant to be some kind of pedantic treatise on biomechanical requirements. I think it was more spiritual or emotional: avoid exaggeration. In the statement 'try to maintain the purity of gaits' the emphasis is not on gaits, it is on purity, stressing the psychological elements that go with it. It is very Zen advice: take the middle path. Dressage, of all the equestrian disciplines, was about making the horse healthier, not breaking him down.

I think the most common fault in riding the pirouette is that the rider uses too much outside rein. This invariably has a braking effect which tends to tip the mass more forward, exactly the opposite of the intentions of the movement. The horse has to understand the back and seat aids so that he learns to gather himself through collection, and then balancing to the rear; the rider guides the movement with weight aids, leaning slightly back and to the inside, while the rider's outside leg encourages the haunches to step under the mass, lift it and push it sideways. (This action is required of the outside hind leg, not the outside foreleg.)

All this talk about exercises, classical interpretation, requirements based on biomechanics, and thoughtful choreography has a very deep and very old philosophical mandate. That is, that the trainer is trying to improve the health and strength of the horse in a natural way. The bias against artifice in the use of exercises, the statement that dressage is not about the fancy paces, is symbolic of the whole relationship with horses. Classical riding is a homage to nature. It is based on mutual respect, not conquest. There must be serious effort not to harm the horse. There is a very dark side to the 'improvements' and evolution of scientific help in riding and training, and this is manifest in the continuous invention and now rampant use of drugs in training dressage horses.

CHAPTER 9

The Dark Side of Science

Marge was an insecure child. She was raised in a wealthy family. Her parents had little time for her. She fell in love with horses early. Her parents supported her hobby; it was a convenient trade-off: they bought off time obligations by giving her horses and letting her spend a lot of time at the stable and in the horse-show life. Marge ate a lot of meals out of vending machines and at horse-show food stands. Over the years she put on a lot of weight and rode less and less. The truth was, she was always a little afraid of riding, and moving more towards ownership over the years was a silky transition. She used her family wealth to buy expensive breeding animals and eventually maintained a showplace farm. She hired and fired a lot of managers over the years and was careful never to relinquish her power to any of them. She legitimately cared about her horses, but she projected much of her own discomfort onto them. She interfered with her trainer's programmes, insisting that certain horses be given time off because of her feelings about things. She wanted the farm to appear peaceful, but was often the cause of a lot of tension.

104

Starting early, her use of pharmacological products was liberal and increasingly exotic.

Lauren was from a lower-middle-class family. She loved animals but especially horses. Her parents could not afford such an affluent indulgence. Lauren was not a physically beautiful child, but she was smart. She studied horses, received scholarships and ended up graduating high in her class at a prominent veterinary school. Over the years, she volunteered in official capacities at horse-shows until she often participated at international competitions. She met a lot of influential owners and trainers. She was clever and had a honed sensitivity to status and social class from being raised on the lower end of it. She managed to ingratiate herself to several powerful competitors. She lectured part-time, and became an expert in drug regulations, their effects and the life expectancies of users. Over time, she worked for the élite of the élite in international competitions; a great deal of her advice involved prescribing medications for élite equine athletes that would not taint the reputations of the users. She became an artist at choice and dosage. The satisfaction she received personally from her indispensability to the wealthiest of the wealthy outweighed her misgivings about the effects on the horses and the dancing around the regulations. Most of the time she could tell herself that the riders would compete the horses anyway, so why not try to relieve their pain, or make them comfortable.

Joseph was sensitive and ambitious. He had trouble with relationships his entire life. He seemed to instinctively and repeatedly seek out liaisons with strong and often unstable personalities. He could not get ahead of the patterns that caused him a lot of anxiety and turmoil in his life. He sought the company of horses for relief from those pressures, but because the pressures were really internal, he didn't realize he carried them along into each situation. The horses often suffered the brunt of his lashing out; he was a screamer, teaching lessons that were abusive. His intensity perversely yielded certain results. The taste of these successes in showing eased the anxiety of his dysfunctional personal life. As he became more adept at competing, because of a certain ferocity fuelled by the deep well of his anger, he seemed to have little trouble using any methods to get ahead of his competitors. He used drugs early in his career and still does. In some cases, it seems so natural to him now that he thinks of them the way most people think of vitamins.

Ronald is a nice guy. He is a good rider, not a great one. His wife is a good manager, which has kept them alive in the horse business. A few years ago he found a sponsor and with the help of that guardian angel he found an exciting horse and they stepped up a big level to some European competitions. He won a few competitions but has never been motivated that way. He gets extremely nervous and, in all his competing over the last few years, he has never been able to go out there without drinking at least half a bottle of wine.

It is usually illegal for drug-makers to sell their products to the general public. Where do lay people get the idea of wanting to try this drug or that? A lot of the time it comes from the advice of doctors who are the only people who can administer these substances. Any product with 'magical' properties will be misused. Doctors are the first step in the responsible monitoring of their applications. It is an impossible job, but it is pretty clearly spelled out for those who choose that life. When there are flagrant abuses they can't be ignored or, worse, accommodated.

These are fictitious people in the examples above. My point is that people use drugs and medical treatments for different complex psychological and sociological reasons. In some cases there are serious causes, but in too many cases they are used with a frightening nonchalance. I think that as much of their abuse comes from misguided kindness as it does from nefarious ambitions.

I feel that, at the bottom of this misguided kindness, is an epidemic laziness in modern horsemen and women which leads to bad riding, and bad riding leads to unnecessary injuries, which lead to all kinds of dramatic medical pyrotechnics.

The hocks and backs of horses seem to have an indelibly strong connection. Many veterinarians will tell you that, if you have a hock problem in a horse, you should look to the back, and if you have a back problem, look to the hocks. Riders won't lose weight and practise correct posture, so they aggravate and injure the backs of their horses. In order to assuage their guilt they obsess on saddle fitting, massage therapy, chiropractic adjustments, every kind of joint supplement, injections and medical treatment.

Too many trainers teach poor position (if they teach it at all). That is assuming they even know what correct position is – many trainers will not take the time and effort to study position. They are afraid that their students will leave them if the work is too hard, so they avoid their responsibility. They let self-esteem override their responsibilities and true education.

They couch their intellectual laziness in nationalistic pride and insecure parochialism. They often defensively harangue and snipe to bully and bluff their way past anyone who questions their flawed knowledge. To them, that is an easier and safer course than going to the books, opening their minds and studying, which is the real hard work of learning dressage. (I think it is very important not to confuse laziness with effort; some people work very hard at being intellectually lazy. To learn takes the courage to let go.) Riders have to remember the advice of de la Guérinière, Podhajsky and so many others who have pointed out that the best riding must be a blend of theory and practice.

Many young trainers get their methods from assorted clinics, often cobbling together ten different systems as if they have equal legitimacy. They torture choreography as if any and all of this work is interchangeable, and their horses and students become more and more confused and frustrated by the inconsistencies and obvious incompatibilities of certain 'schools' of thought. If they do read, they read magazines, the main job of which is to make money by selling advertising. Very often, a publication has to pay more attention to the amount of revenue it receives from advertising than from sales of the magazine to readers. Magazines' goals must be to appeal to the broadest markets for selling advertisers' goods and service, rather than disseminating serious information that may upset customers. Editors seem to have no trouble when articles from one issue to the next contradict each other and contribute to the confusion, not to clarity. Worse still is when they make trendiness, sexiness and superficiality their reason for being.

Real students of riding must take the time and effort to go to source literature and teachers who understand and have experience of these matters. Otherwise, instead of understanding the core principles of straightness and bend, there will just be the passing on of incorrect 'pop' information. When trainers teach things like 'the half-pass is a travers on the diagonal' these may seem like unstudied, innocuous quips, until earnest students try to apply them in practice. When these riders and their horses try to make honest sense of these physical and mental contradictions, they contribute to increasing frustration and nervousness instead of eventual confidence and calm.

Dressage is very hard work. It requires tremendous mental and physical attention that has to be tempered by years of 'deliberate practice'. At the highest levels, it requires extreme controlled effort. These challenges are part of the excitement. In order to be fair, trainers have to be responsible and serious; bad decisions can permanently injure a horse or a rider.

Horses are strong, intelligent, wilful animals. When trainers and writers advise that their training must always be with sugar, they are naïve or romantically selective and ignore the horses' 'thin layer of domestication'; what makes a horse a horse. These facts do not in any way condone abuse, ambition, or a modern version of a prehistoric conquering mentality, tampering with the chemistry of the horse's mind and body. Instead, they require more and more educated judgement, like martial artists who study and sensitize themselves to violence in order to be able to live peacefully. The question will always be: 'Do we have any right to train horses?' Probably we don't, unless our training relationships with horses actually allow us to be trained by the horses as well. This is not a matter of semantics; it has to be a possible fact. I think that if you ride that way, both parties can benefit. Open your mind, tone down your goals, and allow yourself to learn and be taught. Do this at the highest level you can and this approach will respect the horse. The profound respect you may learn from the horses might be their biggest gift to us and the rest of the planet.

CHAPTER 10

Science and Learning

I had a discussion with a student I had taught off and on for a long period. Some of her recent choices had impacted negatively on my own stable and staff. I had to bring this to her attention, along with the fact that I felt her work was deteriorating because of a lack of the right kind of practice. Afterwards, I received a letter from her, the gist of which was that she felt the information was too negative. In her own teaching, she felt it was important to leave the student in an upbeat frame of mind; feeling good about themselves. To that end, she would not take any more lessons and was going to use another instructor. She was reiterating a 'central preoccupation in American culture.'[33]

Jennifer Crocker and Lora E. Park have written an extensive article which appeared in the *Journal of American Psychological Association*, titled 'The Costly Pursuit of Self Esteem'. In the opening paragraph, Crocker and Park mention that the preoccupation with self-esteem can also be seen in the volume of

[33] J. Crocker and L. Park, 'The costly pursuit of self esteem', *Journal of American Psychological Association*, 2004.

scholarly research and writing on the topic. More than 15,000 journal articles on self-esteem have been published over the past thirty years and the interest in this topic has not waned.

Several years ago, I was invited to be a speaker at a meeting of élite swimmers and coaches in British Columbia, Canada. Many of the athletes and coaches had participated at the highest levels of performance in their fields: World Games, Pan Pacific, Olympic Games. I had the opportunity of listening to some fascinating speakers. One of the most significant comments that stuck in my mind was that there was little or no empirical evidence linking self-esteem with performance. To me, the implication was arresting for anyone in the business of training for any kind of performance. It seemed to me that one had better understand the relationship between self-esteem and performance – especially the negative effects that pursuing self-esteem can have on performance.

Crocker and Park noted that people have very definitive beliefs about the importance of self-esteem, yet:

> …a recent and extensive review concluded that high self esteem produces pleasant feeling and enhanced initiative, but does not cause high academic achievement, good job performance or leadership. Nor does low self esteem cause violence, smoking, drinking, taking drugs, or becoming sexually active at an early age. [Furthermore] …in the pursuit of self esteem people often create the opposite of what they need to thrive and … this pursuit has high costs to others as well.[34]

[34] J. Crocker and L. Park, 'The costly pursuit of self esteem', *Journal of American Psychological Association*, 2004.

There are health costs, for as the levels of self-esteem have risen in the last twenty years, so have the levels of anxiety. From my point of view, especially in terms of education and art, the fact that the pursuit of self-esteem can interfere with learning and performance was especially important and not obvious.

I think that many people confuse learning, mastery, and competence. In certain theoretical frameworks aimed at understanding the whole process, competence doesn't necessarily refer to the level of a person's knowledge or skill, but to the ability to adapt and learn from experience. Crocker and Park make the point that: 'The pursuit of self esteem interferes with learning and mastery. When people have self validating goals, mistakes, failures, criticisms and negative feedback are self threats rather than opportunities to learn and improve.'[35]

I know many teachers and coaches in a lot of different fields and the case I cited earlier is not unique. Offended students simply cut off communication and seek another teacher who will hopefully continue to validate their own feelings. Criticism is instantly viewed as self-threat, with accompanying feelings of discomfort. I see more and more of these cases in which there is a perception that any feelings of discomfort are wrong and a rescue system goes immediately into place to restore feelings of well-being and comfort. Unfortunately, a lot of experiences in life are not comfortable and when people use all their effort to restore the good feelings about themselves when anything negative comes along there isn't any room for learning from experience and/or improving simple skills. To quote Crocker and Park once more: 'When people discount, dismiss or excuse their

[35] J. Crocker and L. Park, 'The costly pursuit of self esteem', *Journal of American Psychological Association*, 2004.

mistakes and failures, they are unable to appraise their flaws and shortcomings realistically to identify what they need to learn…There is often some important information or lesson to be learned from negative experiences.'[36]

The reasons why I bring up this subject are twofold: one is the obvious importance of the content; how we can learn to ride better. The other, relating to the scope of this book, is how science helps us to learn: that empirical evidence can help with seemingly immeasurable emotional subjects. Strongly held beliefs do not necessarily have an attachment to strongly documented facts.

The pursuit of knowledge is much more important in the long run and much more practical than the pursuit of self-esteem. To improve any performance, rigorous evaluations of the self are necessary. Bolstering your positions out of defensiveness for egotistical reasons, or to enhance your own sense of well-being, may make you feel better about yourself, but will not make you a better performer or person.

Science and Seeing

Klaus Balkenhol, the current coach of the United States Dressage Team, was also the coach of the German Dressage Team; before that he was a member of a winning German team. He has had a fairly long history of connection to dressage competitions. He has spoken out about judges' apparent drift from the classical principles, in this context, the purity of paces. The FEI rules state:

[36] J. Crocker and L. Park, 'The costly pursuit of self esteem', *Journal of American Psychological Association*, 2004.

The regularity of the paces is fundamental to dressage' [Article 401.8]; 'The trot is a two beat pace of alternate diagonal legs (left fore and right hind legs and vice versa) separated by a moment of suspension' [Article 404.1] and 'The canter is a three beat pace, when in canter to the right, for example, the footfall is as follows: left hind, left diagonal (simultaneously left fore and right hind), right fore, followed by a moment of suspension with all four feet in the air before the next stride begins [Article 405.1].[37]

Balkenhol has commented on photos of several competition horses which show dissociation of gait, in this case in the canter. He says:

Equine biomechanics experts, such as Dr. Hilary Clayton and Dr. Holmström have documented that judges place horses higher which show this type of dissociation of a diagonal pair of legs [the second beat of the canter – my words], the hind foot landing before the front foot. This remains consistent from beginning levels to Grand Prix. [38]

Balkenhol goes on to say that, when comparing a horse with a more three-beat traditional footfall in the extended canter to a seemingly more flamboyant horse, but one with a dissociated (four-beat) canter, 'Two panels of judges at two consecutive World Championships rewarded this [dissociated, flamboyant] canter with a 10. The judges have decided that this canter is ideal.' The obvious irony he has pointed out is that the judges'

[37] FEI descriptions of gaits, *FEI Rules*.
[38] D. Collins, *Dressage Masters*, Lyons Press, 2006.

opinion of a perfect canter completely breaks the rules they are sworn to uphold.

In 1872, Leland Stanford,[39] the railroad tycoon who founded Stanford University in California, tried to settle a debate that had gone on forever. The question was: did a horse at speed have all four feet off the ground? Stanford had a trotting racehorse named Occident and, on his farm in Palo Alto, California, Eadweard Muybridge began his photographic experiments with Occident to crack this visual barrier and settle the matter once and for all. It would take a few more years of refinement of cameras, etc., before Muybridge could bring the exposure time from ½ a second to 1/6,000 of a second. Then, placing twenty-four cameras in a row, he succeeded in proving that a horse does have an airborne phase in the sequence of strides. Science had prevailed, and the study of biomechanics took a big leap forward.

To go back to Balkenhol's criticism, there are legitimate questions. Are judges flagrantly violating their contracts to uphold the rules of the FEI? Or, are they operating under the same limitations of human eyesight that Muybridge exposed in his experiment over 130 years ago?

I personally believe that the FEI rules are noble and in the spirit of classical dressage. Sometimes, new advances in science cloud issues for a while – but it is remarkable to me how well the classical principles have stood up under the scrutiny of ever-evolving science. It would be difficult to argue that the gaits of the dressage horse are totally pure. As gaits have undergone increasingly sophisticated analysis with high-speed films,

[39] W. Beck and H. Clayton, *Equine Locomotion*, W.B. Saunders, Harcourt, 2001.

computers, etc., more variations surface and the less pure the movements seem to be.

On the other hand, it is also clear that some horses are much purer in their movements than others. I have examples of films of different horses in piaffe, trot, etc., which even under slow speed analysis still hold quite close to classic ideals and the FEI requirements. So there are two directions in relationship to the FEI rules: toward or away.

I think Balkenhol's remarks are aimed at the practical application. If judges continue to purposely reward dissociated gaits instead of movement that is more toward the classical ideal, it's clear that competition dressage will move more towards a model like Saddlebred horses and their competitions, where different types of walks, trots, and canters are displayed, and rules will have to be changed.

In this case, I don't believe we are talking about the physical limits of human eyesight so much as lack of guidance from the authorities in competition dressage, based on lack of education. With proper leadership and education it is possible to recognize the extreme distortions and then elucidate why they might not be desirable in the dressage horse in the long run.

I also believe that, from a historical perspective, these tangential drifts toward and away from the classical principles seem to be inevitable. I saw a recent interview with Hans Riegler, a chief rider at the Spanish Riding School. Reigler thought it would take forty years to get back to the classical principles in the dressage community at large. Yet in a way, from his perspective, it wasn't important because the Spanish Riding School and he as a member of it will stay true to the classical principles as they have for 400 years. People will stray but the

Spanish Riding School will remain as a lighthouse when people try to return. [40]

I think his message is important. There is no way to legislate against and control tangential drifts away from the classical principles. You can't even do it with a set of clear and strict rules as with the FEI, especially when vast amounts of money and prestige are involved. However, it is possible that more individual efforts will not only enhance personal integrity but also have a huge impact on the preservation of that art form. I have talked often about how classical dressage has not been preserved by large institutions and the greatest patrons. It has been preserved at times by single individuals in often modest schools, who have held fast to the principles.

[40] S. Loch, (ed.), *The Classical Riding Club Newsletter*, The Classical Riding Club, Spring 2007.

CHAPTER 11

Science, Emotion and Art

The work on understanding the human brain is really just beginning. The neurology of emotions and consciousness is not yet understood. Yet there are advances being made all the time in brain research. Scientists continue to map areas of the brain that are responsible for different activities; in broad areas that handle emotions or intellectual and cognitive analysis, and in specific areas that are activated by the use of a single finger or even the thought of using that finger. In the larger picture, the areas of specialization seem to be fairly fixed, a product of evolutionary strategies. In another sense the most current research shows the brain to be incredibly plastic, with the ability to remap itself for new uses even at advanced ages. As human beings evolved through times of intense fears of predation, the brain had to recognize danger and act quickly in life-threatening situations. The amygdala, one of the oldest and first parts of the brain to develop, was instrumental in accomplishing this; it is the seat of our emotional life. Because of its evolution, it has unique properties which have very modern effects on things like our relationships with people and animals.

Daniel Goleman has stated that:

It was the research work of Joseph Le Doux that proved emotional responses can be initiated directly from the amygdala without information being edited by the more rational neocortex. The conventional models of brain activity had sensory organs transmitting signals to the thalamus and from the thalamus to the neocortex where these signal are sorted out, and instructions are issued for the appropriate responses.[41]

With Le Doux's work we see, according to Daniel Goleman, how anatomically the emotional system can act independently of the neocortex and how this 'circuitry does much to explain the power of emotion to overwhelm rationality'.

How many of us have endured or been responsible for emotional tirades in riding lessons? These are clear cases of inappropriate, childlike emotional responses often coming from seemingly highly trained, sophisticated, intellectual people. Although the brain circuitry can explain this phenomenon, it cannot excuse it.

There is some very interesting and exciting work in the field of neuroplasticity. Richard Davidson has, for years now, worked with some Tibetan Buddhist monks who are experts in meditation. What do 2,000 years of practice of meditation have to do with the most current work in neuroplasticity? It seems

[41] D. Goleman, *Emotional Intelligence*, Bantam Books, 1995.

that when Davidson recorded their brain activity with sophisticated MRIs, the monks were capable of – at will – flooding and exciting areas in the brain responsible for things like compassion far beyond the capability of any normal people. What scientists were discovering was that purposeful training of the mind could alter activity of the brain – which had been thought to be 'hard-wired' and out of our control.[42] In fact, there was no physiological reason why people needed to surrender to inevitable 'floods' of emotion. The emotional aspects of our mentality are as trainable as the intellectual aspects.

As we evolve, it has become increasingly necessary to involve more mental training and editing of our first-defence emotional reactions. One of the plagues of Western culture is the extreme bias toward intellectual achievements and an embarrassing discomfort with emotional achievements. Primitive taboos still surround mental health today and support an uncultured shyness around the whole area of emotional development. These attitudes stunt completeness in our lives and cement a lifetime of imbalance.

For us especially in the West, as science seems to authenticate 2,000 years of dressage practice towards collection, science also seems to be authenticating 2,000 years of spiritual practice in the East toward another form of collection. The challenge that each of us has, is to somehow transpose this information into the action of our own lives.

It is wonderful when the science is on time to answer you questions: when Muybridge can find out if a horse is airborne. Even for the magnificent Dalai Lama, Tenzin Gyatso, to see

---

[42] S. Begley, *Train Your Mind Change Your Brain*, Ballantine Books, 2007.

validation of his efforts and those of his teachers. However, most times the science comes at its own speed. Most scientists live without knowing. How do you live an authentic life when you don't know?

One of the biggest gifts of art is that artists study, suspend and manipulate emotions. How much of art is the creation of tangible models of emotional and intellectual experiences? Artists can take emotions and feeling out of the speed and immediacy of real time and let us practise our responses. I don't think that artists necessarily revel in controlling emotions or controlling a life that creates emotions. Rather, art lets us examine our reactions to life outside its speed. A great play lets us react to a family tragedy, while a babysitter safely watches our own children. Listening to a symphony can repeatedly elicit certain emotions whenever we are ready for them, or we can turn it off if we are not. Art can suspend the pressure of real grief, slow down that tension of real fear, and extend the ecstasy of real joy.

We have always looked to artists to interpret, explore and expose the emotional part of our brain and lives. Even today, neuroscientists defer to the poets at times. M. Pollan put this in the following terms: 'We don't yet understand consciousness scientifically, so how can we hope to explain changes in consciousness scientifically... I'm afraid we have to leave these questions still to the poets.'[43]

Artists help us to learn how we respond to ourselves. In the end, you don't need a literary critic to tell you how to respond to a writer. You don't need a dressage judge to tell you how to respond to a rider and horse. You have to find out for yourself.

[43] M. Pollan, *The Botany of Desire*, Random House, 2001.

Artists have always shied away from explanations of a reviewer's response to their work. They consistently respect that relationship between their art and another person as personal between the viewer and the work, and out of their control.

As we have seen, you can use the sciences of personalities to find clues about what kind of person you are; how you like to learn. You can use art to practise your emotional reactions. However, the real art of living will be to define yourself first-hand with your own experiences. These experiences, your own experiences, will tell your story. As your story unfolds, you may feel you don't fit this genealogy or that taxonomic category. You find that you can't accept that propaganda, or you don't believe this religion. You don't seem to be fulfilling other people's expectations. Yet in all this disassembly, you don't feel lost because you are becoming something else, the person you really are. And when you find out who you are, you begin to know what you are supposed to do. Finding your own path, you become yourself.

Index

125

communication, in horses 23–5
competence 113
competitive dressage 34, 39, 52–3
   judges 71–2, 114–17
conformation of horse 77
contact 47, 73–6
contradictions, in training 66–8
control of horse 54–6
crest 60–1
criticism 113
Crocker, Jennifer 111–14

da Vinci, Leonardo 69
dance 83
Davidson, Richard 120–1
de Pluvinel, Antoine 13, 40–2
de Waal, F. 25
discomfort 113
dominance, in horses 13–14, 18–19,
   22, 25
drugs, use of 104–7
The Dynamic Horse 78–9

ears, horses' 23–4
elegance 86–7
Emotional Intelligence 38
emotions, human 119–23
engagement 59, 77–9, 80–1
ethics 109
exercises
   choreography of 86–7, 88–9
   evolution 82
   half-pass 90–3
   longitudinal 93–7
   piaffe 97–9
   shoulder-in 78–86
   travers and renvers 87–90
external validation 11–12, 39
eyes, horses' 24
eyesight, horses' 23

failures 113–14
feeding, anticipation 28
'feel'
   collection 63–4, 96
   flying changes 100–1
   shoulder-in 85
FEI dressage rules 114–15, 116
feral horses, behaviour 14–25
fighting, in horses 18–19, 21
fishing line, test 75–6

Flehman gesture 18, 24
flexions, jaw/neck 55
'flow' 38–9
flying changes 100
foals 24
force, use of 22
forehand
   elevation 36, 62, 70, 98
   see also on the forehand
forelegs, upward forces of 46–8, 93–5
France, classical riding 40–2
front end, horses 59–62

gaited horses 84, 117
gaits
   early photographic experiments
     116
   FEI rules 114–15, 116
   rhythm and purity 101–2, 115–17
Garner, Howard 72
Goleman, Daniel 38, 120
grooming, mutual 24
ground reaction forces
   collection 70–1, 95
   half-pass 93
   piaffe 48–50

half-pass 90–3
handling, of horses 26–7
hands
   lightness of 73–6
   positioning of 67–8
Hawaii 7–10
head, horse's
   natural use of 24
   ridden position/carriage 34–5
   see also neck, horse's
hearing, horses' sense of 23
hierarchies, horse groups 13–14
hind legs, engagement 59, 77–9, 80–1
hindquarters, horses' 58–9
   weight shift to 36, 70–1, 98
hock action 78–81
hocks, connection with back 107
hormones, horses' 18
horse-rider, as one system 56
Hot Air Balloon 18–19
human brain 39, 119–21
human-horse relationships 13–14,
   109–10